Take Five

Best Contemporary Tanka

Volume 4

Take Five

Best Contemporary Tanka

Volume 4

2011

Edited by

M. Kei, editor-in-chief (United States)
Patricia Prime (New Zealand)
Magdalena Dale (Romania)
Amelia Fielden (Australia/Japan)
Claire Everett (United Kingdom)
Owen Bullock (New Zealand)
David Terelinck (Australia)
Janick Belleau (Canada)
David Rice (United States)

Keibooks
Perryville, Maryland, USA
2012

Keibooks

P O Box 516, Perryville, MD, 21903, USA
<http://AtlasPoetica.org>

Take Five : Best Contemporary Tanka, Volume 4
Copyright © 2012 M. Kei

ISBN 978-0615597805

Acknowledgments

The editors wish to thank the many editors, poets, and fans who submitted books, chapbooks, journals, websites, photocopies, PDFs, transcripts, music, recordings, videos, and other materials for our perusal. This year we reviewed over 180 venues and eighteen thousand poems. Without their support it would have been impossible.

Table of Contents

Introduction: The Pity of Things

The Pity of Things

Part I

As I edited this year's selection of tanka, I noticed the short list was filled with tanka expressing sadness, loss, and lament. This is not unusual; *aware*, the Japanese concept of transience, has always been a hallmark of tanka. It is an essential element of Japanese aesthetics to notice and appreciate the perishability of the world. Partly this comes from Buddhism, and partly from Nature, as the natural and spiritual worlds decay and are renewed. This year the influence seemed especially strong, and I can't help wondering if the editorial team's awareness that this will be the last volume of *Take Five* subconsciously influenced our decisions.

I know that I have been keenly aware of the ending of the project; about eighteen months ago I became very ill to the point that I could no longer sail. Anyone who knows me will appreciate the significance of that loss. For much of the next year, I was barely able to function and was in and out of the emergency room and doctors' offices. At first I thought I would soon be over my illness and could carry on with *Take Five*, but as my illness extended to the point of collapse, I realized that would be impossible. Thus I made the decision to end the series.

Take Five is a unique and powerful project, and I did not feel reducing its scope or limiting its nature would do justice to the tradition of inclusion and thoroughness that has made it unique. For four years, the editorial teams have scoured all manner of resources from journals to books to websites to musical scores to live performances to art project—even advertisements—in order to discover and appreciate the vast variety of tanka and related literature published in English. This year we read over eighteen thousand poems and consulted more than 180 venues. We managed to read ninety-seven percent.

In 2011, tanka found expression in everything from print to orchestral music. In addition to the sponsoring of tanka performances by museums and other venues, we are also seeing an increasing use of YouTube for video publication of chapbooks and poetry readings. Pentti Olavi Syrjälä of Finland has made the greatest number of publications via YouTube, but he is not alone. Professional musicians continue to seek inspiration in tanka, the latest being Erik Spangler with his composition *Five Levels of the Watershed*, a tone poem for orchestra. Poets on Site continues producing its multi-disciplinary arts programs in California, and the *One World, Many Voices*, a fundraiser in the wake of the disaster in Japan, presented Japanese poetry forms, including tanka.

The earthquake, tsunami, and nuclear disaster in the spring of 2011 had a profound impact. Many Japanese poets were directly affected, while poets elsewhere were stunned by the disaster unfolding in the home of tanka. Working as an editor, I could not reach some poets and was told by those who knew them, "She lived in Sendai." Sometimes that news was followed weeks later with notice that the poet was safe with friends, but on other occasions, "Still no news."

Some of the most affecting poems were written by Japanese gogyohka poets who were eyewitnesses to the disaster, and who, in the days and weeks of the aftermath, put pen to paper to express their feelings. These were published in a special feature in *Flashquake,* an online journal of short literary forms. 'Gogyohka' is a Japanese form derived from tanka, but it abandons the syllable count of traditional tanka. Gogyohka are equivalent to tanka in English in that they are written on five lines with due considerations for breath and aesthetics, but no requirements for the number of syllables. Although tanka and gogyohka in Japanese are quite different from each other, gogyohka and tanka in English are indistinguishable. English-language tanka gave up syllable-counting long ago because the languages are so different; a thirty-one syllable poem in English did not convey the elusive and fragmentary nature of the originals. The gogyoshi poem derived from gogyohka has even fewer rules.

Take Five has never attempted to define tanka; instead we take it as we find it. Any poem, regardless of what label is put on it by a poet, editor, or journal, is eligible, provided it meets the basic criteria of five poetic parts. This encompasses waka, kyoka, gogyohka, gogyoshi, and nonce forms as well. It is not necessary for the poem to be written on five lines (although most are); likewise, the mere fact that a short poem is written on five lines does not make it a tanka—limericks are not tanka. It is a founding belief of *Take Five* that by presenting a wide array of poetry, we enrich the genre and recognize and stimulate the creative endeavors of the authors.

This year we noted a number of fine pieces of tanka prose were published and attempted to expand our selection of tanka prose pieces. However, due to limits of space and budget, it is not possible to do justice to the field of long tanka poetry, including tanka prose, tanka sequences, responsive tanka, and shaped tanka. Readers are encouraged to seek out the journals that do publish long works, such as *Haibun Today, Atlas Poetica,* and *Lynx.* Although several of the print journals publish short sequences and tanka prose, only *Atlas Poetica* is of sufficient size to publish long sequences. The field of long tanka is therefore largely in the hands of online journals and websites. We believe the time is ripe for another anthology of long tanka; the last one was *The Tanka Prose Anthology* in 2008.

Changes continue in the world of tanka. Several new journals, *Multiverses, A Hundred Gourds, Haiku Bindii,* and *Ardea,* have joined the field to publish Japaniform poetry. *Ardea* is a multilingual, international journal. *Chrysanthemum* and *Simply Haiku* emerged from hiatus to publish again. *Haiku Bindii* proved to be a very strong new forum with numerous nominations from its pages.

Jeffrey Woodward, long time editor of *Haibun Today,* announced new editorial staff for each department. He will serve as managing editor. Deborah Kolodji, long time co-editor of *Dwarf Stars,* the speculative fiction short poetry anthology, has moved on to a new venture, *Eye to the Telescope,* a journal devoted to the same. *Jars of Stars,* one of many attempts to curate Twitter poetry, ceased operating in 2011.

Magnapoets published two new anthologies, *Butterfly Away* and *Many Windows*. Poets on Site published several anthologies, including the *Pacific Asia Museum's 40th Anniversary Audio Tour,* as well as *On Awakening, Alchemy,* and *Painted My Way.* MET Press published *Dreams Wander On : Contemporary Poems of Death Awareness,* the only anthology from MET Press this year. Koyama Press of France published two anthologies, *Anemones* and *Garden Mandala.* Australia continues its tanka development, publishing the anthologies *Grevillea and Wonga Vine : Australian Tanka Poetry of Place,* and *Food for Thought.* Anthology publications were light compared to previous years, and the team hopes the reduced publications of former stalwarts of the field does not bode ill.

In good news, this year saw publication of two items of special interest to educators: Terry Ann Carter edited an anthology entitled *Lighting the Global Lantern,* an anthology of Japanese short form poetry and nonfiction, especially intended for teaching teenage and young adult students. *Atlas Poetica* offered a special feature online, '25 Tanka for Children (and Educators)' aimed at students age 5-12, marking the first such resource made available for this age group. It is accompanied by a generous Educational Use Policy. The *Tanka Teachers Guide*, first published in 2007 by the MET Press, is still available, and TankaOnline.com publishes educational material for tanka poets. Jane Reichhold revised and reorganized her various essays into the 'School of Wind Five-Folded Tanka,' published at AHA Poetry. Jeffrey Woodward founded the Tanka Prose Forum, a workshop dedicated to tanka prose, the first time that a forum has been dedicated specifically to that purpose.

Non-fiction publishing in the form of literary criticism and book reviews continues with the bulk being published in *Haibun Today* and *Atlas Poetica*. Shorter articles and reviews appear in other journals, such as *Ribbons* and *Kokako*. Topics discussed in 2011 included gogyohka and gogyoshi, tanka prose, Catalan tanka, personal journeys in writing tanka prose, and other items. Charles Tarlton has emerged as an important new author of tanka criticism, while Patricia Prime continues as a major reviewer of tanka books. Momentum built through the year for both book reviews and articles and continues into the early months of 2012.

Print publication dropped off sharply for 2011. Although the number of venues reviewed was slightly higher than last year, the number of print publications plummeted to almost half of what it had been in previous years. Anthologies were much fewer in number. The difference was made up by blogs, websites, web journals, and other electronic media. Forty percent of books containing tanka published in 2011 appeared as e-books, either as an accompaniment to the print edition, or as a standalone e-book.

Two dozen titles that had previously appeared in print were reissued as e-books in PDF format via print-on-demand publisher Lulu Enterprises, but complaints about quality and service prompted one small tanka press, Keibooks, to move to CreateSpace. Most of the reprints had been reviewed by previous *Take Five* teams in their original print editions, so were not eligible this year. New books containing tanka were also published as Kindle Editions via Amazon Digital

Services, but the editorial team learned about these too late to read them. This is the first time Kindle has been a significant presence in tanka publishing, although tanka published elsewhere has been retailed through Amazon. Smashwords.com published a handful of books containing tanka, but since Smashwords doesn't even have 'poetry' as a category (the only options are 'Fiction' and 'Non-fiction'), this independent ebook publisher is not a good fit for tanka poets. Scribd.com, once a repository for archival copies of previously published tanka books and journals, saw little new development, although a few previously unknown poets published on the site.

Formerly prolific presses, such as MET Press, AHA Poetry, and Poets on Site, were much reduced over previous years. In addition, there was a reduction in self-publishing via print-on-demand (POD) printers. Smaller presses, such as Eucalypt, Keibooks, Black Cat Press, Koyama Press, Winfred Press, and Magnapoets continued operating at their usual levels. In some cases, the decline is attributable to the health problems of the publishers (Denis Garrison at MET Press, M. Kei at Keibooks), but in other cases, it is presumed that the declining economy discouraged poets from self-publishing, or encouraged them to seek out cheaper alternatives, such as ebook and online publishing.

Thus, although the overall publishing has maintained steady, a seismic shift to electronic publication has occurred. In part this reflects the energies of talented individuals who published in print no longer being able to commit the same amount of time and energy as before, but it also speaks to the importance of building relationships between readers and poets that is so valuable and so readily facilitated by social media. Several poets have spoken to me about how much they prefer Twitter because of the instant feedback it gives them and the friendly relationships they enjoy with readers. Several of them commented that they have mostly given up on print publications, or that they have to push themselves to submit to traditional media. Thus it seems that a combination of economics and access is driving the move to electronic publishing.

The gatekeeping role once performed by conventional media has ceased to have any utility. Those editors who are most prolific and have the steadiest, most reliable publication schedules, are those who look at themselves as partners in support of poets, not those who presume to dictate what tanka is or isn't. Promulgations that tanka "must" have a pivot, or "have" to be formatted as short-long-short-long-long, or "ought" to be written like a haiku with two lines of subjective commentary tacked on, have ceased to have any real meaning. With the ability of poets to publish whatever they wish via social media, blogs, email lists, ebooks, and other electronic sources, those who don't agree with any given editorial dictate are able to publish and garner significant readerships without having to pass an editorial litmus test. This probably constitutes one of the largest breaks with Japanese tradition; in Japan tanka is still taught in tanka poetry circles by tanka masters who critique student work (including the work of students who have been writing and publishing for decades), and who decide what gets published in their journals. Although the Japanese method of teaching tanka has had only limited impact on Anglophone tanka poets, it has had even less impact on social media poets. This more than anything indicates that tanka written in English is a separate genre. Although it originated in Japanese and retains important connections, especially with regards to aesthetics, the genie is out of the bottle.

Part II

One of the most commented upon images this year was a news photograph of a young girl being checked with a radiation detector in Fukushima in the wake of the disaster in Japan. This image cropped up in various poems published throughout the year, and one in particular appears in *Take Five*:

> so proud
> a girl on the front page—
> the camera watching her
> a radiation detector
> sweeping over her tiny body

Naoko Kishigami Selland

It's difficult to grapple with such an enormous disaster in five short lines, but this tanka by Selland manages to capture the tragedy. David Rice explains, "It's hard to write a poem about a nuclear power plant melt down that avoids both intellectualized detachment and emotional over-involvement. The middle three lines, mainly nouns and verbs, describe the photograph. It is the adjectives in the first and last lines that bring the picture to life. The girl is proud, which highlights the incongruity between her childhood pride at having her picture taken for the newspaper and the larger context that she may have received a dose of radiation sufficient to cause cancer.

"The poignancy of her naivete reverberates until stopped by the second-to-last word, 'tiny.' It is not just that the girl is naïve. She also is incapable of doing anything to change her fate, and we are tiny in the face of catastrophes, too. We also are naïve in our assumption that, if a catastrophe happens where we live, we and the people we love will magically escape. 'We are all Japan' we said to each other after the tsunami. This poem brought the Japanese tragedy home to me."

It is never easy to choose which poems will make it into the final anthology; this year's crop of poems was particularly hard to choose among. Perhaps it was the burden of knowing that this is the last volume in the *Take Five* series, or perhaps it was the triple disaster in Japan that made the ephemeral shimmers we call 'tanka' seem so fragile. Perhaps it was my own health troubles that made me feel old. In any event, the poem that resonated with me was:

> an old hag
> bent over a shoulder bag
> in the shop's window
> I straighten my spine before
> they can see it was me

Linda Jeannette Ward

Like Ward, I feel bent, old, and haggard; the glimpses of myself in the mirror are not how I imagine myself to be. It is a Dorian Gray moment that reveals our sins in the image, a moment that partakes more of Faust than of classical tanka. Yet our sins are petty and have not been magnified by anything as dramatic as a deal with the Devil. Unfortunately, where there is no damnation, there is also no hope of salvation. We are left adrift in the cockleboat of our lives. We must make sense of ourselves at an age where there is a great deal of evidence about exactly who we are and what we have accomplished (or failed to accomplish), and very little time left to change it. Still, in spite of our feebleness, we don't want anyone else to see us this way, so we straighten and pretend it wasn't us in the looking glass.

No matter what we do, Death comes to all of us, the innocent and guilty alike:

clouds cast
shadows on the lake
and pass—
his coffin was white
and three feet long

Edith Bartholomeusz

Editor Claire Everett says, "However many times I read this tanka, I can't fail to be brought up with a jolt by those final two lines. The scene is calm, light, an every day experience, yet these clouds don't leave reflections, they leave shadows. Some lives are so brief, they are little more than cloud shadows. However we might try to come to terms with the impermanence of this existence, from time to time, there are those reminders that we are all hostages to fortune, that terrible things happen over which we have no control. In a moment of reflection, daydream, perhaps, the poet remembers this lost child. The stark image of the closing lines stays with me, as a reader, evoking the way in which this experience has impacted on the poet and will continue to for the remainder of her own life."

The passage of time and its mortal significance are on the mind of many of us, and Cherie Hunter Day's poem is one of many on the theme:

> a brown moth
> folded on the windowsill
> an expiration date
> on my cereal box—
> as if I needed reminders

Cherie Hunter Day

David Terelinck comments, "Cherie Hunter Day presents us with an extraordinary tanka through observation of ordinary images of everyday life. Her tanka takes us from the external and mirrors this on a personal level. Immediately we are drawn to not just a moth, but a brown moth. Such definitive use of this colour immediately draws us into an ageing world; a place where autumn, a loss of vitality, and death are easily courted. And this moth, although no longer alive, is simply "folded" on the windowsill. As if it has died in the routine of daily life, much as we might one day go when folding the linen and putting away the weekly wash.

"And the expiration on the cereal box: so many little deaths that would normally go unnoticed or unrecorded until seen in ourselves. "as if I need reminders"—but we all do; because we so often get caught up in the mundane of life, getting breakfast for our spouse or children, doing the laundry, going to work . . . Sometimes in existing we forget to live. Cherie's poem reminds us of this. It is a mental and emotional prod that we too are finite, and have an expiry date which will creep up upon us unless we are vigilant and live our lives to the fullest advantage."

Death and memory are on Owen Bullock's mind as he addresses two tanka in the anthology:

> the nurse says
> you'd better come now—
> in the winter dawn
> a wisp of cloud
> floats across the moon

Hannah Mahoney

"It almost doesn't matter what the second part of this tanka records. The fact is that we remember what's going on round us in the moment after we receive tragic news. Yes, it's winter, and death, of various kinds, is not far away. Yes, a wisp of cloud moves across the face of the moon, as of the spirit that will soon pass. But there is light yet, perhaps of a life well-lived."

> is it still
> their anniversary
> if one
> has gone and the other
> doesn't remember?

Ruth Holzer

"Initially, I think one tends to have a strong reaction and say, 'no, how can it be'. But a yes answer to the question may settle in after long and hard consideration. It is still their anniversary to the loved ones around those concerned. Does this matter much? Maybe it matters even less to the wider community. But someone notices: the poet. She notices for them, in the same way one does things for the sick or aged who can no longer look after themselves fully. I'd suggest that this poem is all about remembrance."

Remembering comes with a price. Janick Belleau points out, "A scourge of society has not been eradicated notwithstanding constant work of consciousness raising of pressure groups: physical and psychological violence against women and children. Sometimes, violence leaves 'broken bones' and often, a wounded heart; often, it leaves 'unseen scars' and sometimes, they 'can be seen for miles.'"

    when I was eight
    he threw the car keys
    at my mother . . .
    on clear blue days
    the scar can be seen for miles

    Andrew Riutta

    cut out of the will
    all he ever left me
    was a legacy
    of broken bones
    and unseen scars

    Tracy Davidson

Patricia Prime finds redemption in the transience of the world through the numinous nature of language.

"Brian Zimmer's tanka is a luminous poem about loss. This seems to me an impressionistic sketch with a touch of an epiphany about it—at a very ordinary level. There is a special dimension of reverence in his poem, yet at the same time the earthbound image of 'the white rose' grounds the poem in the here and now. Instead of saying 'petals fall' he uses the word 'unpetal'—that's poetry. It's a kind of compression that incorporates a spectrum of a response into a single noun that suggests his language is alive. And unless the language is trying to get off the page in some way, then it becomes merely description."

the white rose
unpetals
at my touch
even death's perfection
fleeting

Brian Zimmer

Owen Bullock develops the theme of transience and timelessness further in his commentary on Dawn Bruce's tanka prose, 'Pursuit.'

"The ghosts and shadows of the opening sentence of Dawn Bruce's tanka prose suggest complexity, and lend the writing an air of mystery. The work is poetically enigmatic, the metaphor 'our life was lemon-ginger tea' is an example of this tone. The word 'drifts' in that first tanka hints at the characters' state of mind: in love, there's a sense of timelessness; they are in their own world.

"The writer's new name is stressed, and the *undistinguished* quality of the neighbourhood emphasises their need to get away. Personally, I can relate to the comments about entertainment. As I get older, I find that entertainment isn't entertaining any more and looking out the window or doing everyday things make for a kind of emotional plenum. This couple's activities complement one another, whilst still being individual.

"When they want a change and go camping, their needs are again simple. The mention of *unspoilt* nature perhaps has something to do with the way they'd like to be. And they take delight in each other: she cooks to please him, he makes a garden to please her. If, overall, elements of this work are exaggerated for effect, dramatised or romanticised, they hold true. The closing tanka, like the first, is distinct from the prose and captures a moment, in fine haiku style, when their chosen isolation is interrupted."

David Rice addresses the isolation and anxiety that can happen even while we are still alive and in the midst of our families when he comments on this poem by Lisa Alexander Baron:

Flightless beetles
with useless wings sealed
beneath wing covers—
my daughter tells me
I worry too much

Lisa Alexander Baron

"This beetle species once could fly but now is flightless. The mother-daughter relationship also has evolved. Now that her daughter is older and eager to take flight, the poet sees potential dangers, but all she can do is worry. And there is another layer. The mother was once the daughter. Once she was setting out into the world and her mother was the one worrying 'too much.' The repetitions in the first three lines, flightless and useless, wings and wings, emphasize the mother's inability to get her daughter to listen to her. The link and shift between a flightless beetle and a mother-daughter relationship lets the reader feel what parents feel when their cautionary advice cannot penetrate the insouciance of their children. Here is the power of tanka realized."

What redeems the anxiety, the worry, the loneliness, and the transience of the world, is love. Plenty of poets in the volume give us love in all its forms.

> this former lover
> has slipped back into the cracks
> in my life
> what happens next,
> mid-winter sun

Peggy Heinrich

Amelia Fielden speaks to the sense of wonder that love can instill in anyone of any age.

"Peggy's tanka conveys a delightful sense of excitement and wonder, which anyone on their own, particularly over a 'certain age,' can relate to. In this one small poem, there are two excellent metaphors: 'slipped back into the cracks/in my life' . . . yes, there are 'cracks,' even in the best ordered and most self-sufficient life; and 'mid-winter sun,' unexpected but blissful when it arrives. The third line, 'in my life, is a clever and smooth pivot: with this pivot, the tanka can be read as two three-lined poems 'this former lover/ had slipped back into the cracks/ in my life'; and 'in my life/what happens next/mid-winter sun'."

The most unabashed paeans to love come from our Romanian contributors. Love in the English-speaking world is often fraught with a world-weary acknowledgement of pain and suffering, but in the tanka of Romanian poets, love survives as that giddy, naive delight that believes everything is possible—even happy endings.

Magdalena Dale gives particular attention to two poets from Romania:

Lan galben de grâu—
cu flori de mac în braţe
şi-n părul fluturând.
Cum eu nu am curajul
te mângâie doar vântul.

Golden field of wheat—
you have poppies in your arms
and in your fluttering hair.
As I don't have the courage
just the wind is hugging you.

Jules Cohn Botea

"Jules Cohn Botea is in *Take Five* for the first time. I like his tanka for the image of his graceful love feeling. The wind that plays in the beloved person's hair, but he doesn't dare to touch it seems to be like in the old poems of love written for the ladies of the Japanese Imperial court and it sounds like a love letter. I like this suggestion of deep love so much because I think it is more powerful than to say love directly which is too much used."

Ridic ciutura
să strâng cu mâna căuş
stele bob cu bob—
când vii la ceas de taină
le prefir în calea ta.

Water in the well
with my palm I skim the pail
to catch stars one by one—
when in the night you visit
I scatter them before you.

Vasile Smărăndescu

"Vasile Smărăndescu is also in *Take Five* for the first time. I like the poetic image when you are in love to gather the stars from the sky and scatter them before the beloved person. There are so many stars and so many explosive feelings when we are in love and he would like to share all his joy of love and life with us. This poem is highly emotive, conjures strong visual/sensory images that can be contemplated again and again. It manages to contain the love universe in five short lines."

The editors of *Take Five* have brought this fourth and final volume to a satisfying conclusion. It contains almost four hundred individual tanka and several pieces of tanka prose and sequence, making it the single largest volume in the series and a fitting capstone.

We are indebted to Japan for giving us a world of short poetry forms, such as haiku, senryu, waka, tanka, kyoka, gogyohka, gogyoshi, and numerous variations, and we were challenged by the triple disaster in Japan to look beyond the limits of our own lives and experiences. Melding Japanese aesthetics with our own Western minimalist tradition of "less is more," we were able to grasp the immensity of the loss and transform it into words. Each poem, like a lantern set alight on the misty sea, is a beacon crossing between this world and the next. The tanka and its five line relatives are both transient and timeless. So tiny, so fragile, so ephemeral, they begin and end in a breath, and yet, like delicate seashells, they are made of durable material that long outlasts the creatures that made them.

Let us incise tanka on pottery, carve it on stone, embroider it on cloth, and engrave it on metal. Paint it, build it, weave it, make it tangible and leave it behind. Poems are the grave-goods of poets. They are worth nothing if they are kept concealed in our hearts; it is only by sharing them that we can enrich the world around us. A human life is no more durable than paper, but a poem lives forever.

M. Kei
Editor-in-chief, *Take Five : Best Contemporary Tanka*, Volume 4

Individual Tanka

Adelaide B. Shaw

if I could turn back
I'd revise some stories
of my life,
yet, the part in which you come
would always be the same

Akiko Hasegawa

a bunch of daffodils
shines like a torch
in the empress's hand—
those flowers
from the tsunami wasteland

Alan S. Bridges

halfway through spring
a hummingbird
loses itself
finds itself
in the columbine

Alan Summers

sometimes
before falling in love
with my wife
again and again
the cries of swifts

Alex von Vaupel

at night the hospice
fills with urgent whispers
to the moon
"i am not ready yet
to sleep forever"

Alexander Ask

white quartz stone
carrying a glint
in jagged edges
the hope of seeing you
without the other man

Alexis Rotella

I left before I fell
from his pedestal—
too hard
pretending to be
marble

Up before dawn—
someone or something
is knocking on the wall . . .
it could be the rain
or it could be Death

Alison Williams

how many things
do I need to dispose of
before
each one left
becomes precious?

Amelia Fielden

capricious spring
dark clouds and scudding wings
just when
the flowers and I
felt ready to bloom

from Europe
your daytime calling
my deep night,
our voices making love
along the seabed

she leaned there
against the persimmon tree
waving goodbye—
neither of us said
see you next time

the corsages
that man always brought her
cream gardenias
how I hated the scent
of her betrayals

André Surridge

from a hilltop
we watch mist in the valley
disappear . . .
one day that will be me
says grandfather

Andrew Riutta

when I was eight
he threw the car keys
at my mother . . .
on clear blue days
the scar can be seen for miles

Angela Leuck

alone in the house
after you've gone
in the silence
I scrape layer after layer
of paint from an old chair

in an old picture
my mother's hand so firm
on my shoulder
as if gravity alone
could not hold me down

he always knows
the words to hurt me—
I put on my boots
to close the gate
the wind has blown open

walking home
in November mist
the weight
in my hand
of one red rose

Angie LaPaglia

crouching by the fire
sorting by size
and shape
the thoughts of you
I've gathered

the weight
of silence
my thin hips bear
another
childless morning

Anita Virgil

primordial soup
this love of ours
primitive and wild
we create a universe
as the stars whiz by

Anne Benjamin

a simple sack
filled with daily rice
stitched tight
I wish you could find
the thread to release me

this morning
my coffee smells so good
and tastes so bitter—
you call me by my name
still do not know me

an'ya

an icy wind
and bits of sparkle expose
the evergreens
anchored by their tap roots
unlike you unlike me

together may we
hear violins in the rain . . .
for without love
all sounds are unbearable
in that silence called absence

cold cemetery
the long sleeves of your old coat
warm my fingertips
even from beyond this grave
you manage to comfort me

Antoinette Libro

overnight ferry
from Naples to Palermo
the sea sings us to sleep—
I dream of grandmother's name
on the ship's manifest

Askold Skalsky

passes me in the hall
with barely a nod
if she only knew
what we did last night
in my dream

Autumn Noelle Hall

Chinese characters
brush-stroked in canine nose prints
on my rear window
at last my dog is speaking
a language I can translate

Aubrie Cox

the silence between us
grows deeper
from the backseat
our daughter hums
a love song

summer leaves
already falling
when the music dies
in me, will I know
it's time to move on?

Audrey Olberg

arriving home each night
you always hug the dog
    before you come
    into the kitchen
    and don't hug me

at last—
moving in together
      her tampons
      on his side
of the medicine chest

Aya Yuhki

the river in the shade
of thick-leaved cherry trees—
drawing
the souls of the dead,
fireflies' blue lights shimmer

Barbara Robidoux

midnight drive home
a star fell from the sky
opening
the silence
between us

Barbara A. Taylor

a grateful mother
thanks her grateful daughter
in the cancer ward . . .
now I keep wondering
who will hold my hand

Barry Goodmann

low tide
the shipwreck
emerges
I find the words
to say I was wrong

Beatrice van de Vis

opening a window
in the stillness before dawn
to let the moon in—
as if it could comfort me
in his far away absence

Becky Alexander

sickle moon
slices the midnight sky . . .
some wounds
too deep
for healing

Belinda Broughton

generations
of young men
like this one
throwing stones
at the military tank

Bett Angel-Stawarz

crushed eucalypt
wafting on a breeze—
your aroma
rising on the steam
as I iron your shirt

Bette Norcross Wappner

from the eaves
sheets of snow are falling
this winter solstice
our own little avalanche
over a black negligee

Beverley George

it's not the new
that makes me cry at weddings
but the borrowed veil
the time-worn words,
and old couples holding hands

passages you marked
with pressed grasses
scribbled notes . . .
what were those deep thoughts
you presumed I did not share

this blue balloon—
how far has it travelled
to bob down in my garden?
on it, *love from mummy
to Will . . . age five . . . in heaven*

Beverly Acuff Momoi

the cat retreats
to the corner of the closet
deep within the dark
how often
I choose silence

the magnolia's
leathery leaves in winter
evergreen . . .
four years after her stroke
her laugh still strong

Bob Lucky

a beggar
follows me across the road
when I turn
to make him go away
he hands me the pen I dropped

Bob Lucky

Gerd Börner, Dietmar Tauchner, Klaus-Dieter Wirth, German-English translators

prayer flags
color the breeze
conversations
we might have had
seem possible again

Gebetsfahnen
farben die Brise
Gesprache
die wir gehabt haben konnten
scheinen wieder moglich

Brendan Slater

a mattress
on a concrete floor
since I sold my bed
no one comes to visit me
not even in my dreams

in this foreign land
I'm a beggar of words
another day ends
and my cap's full to the brim
with buttons and bottle tops

Brian Zimmer

the white rose
unpetals
at my touch
even death's perfection
fleeting

Byakuren Yanagihara

Harue Aoki, Japanese-English Translator

bloom and fall,
life is just simple—
I mentioned
to a maiden
falling in love

C. William Hinderliter

winter fog
strolling in the darkness
past the old church ruins
I suddenly notice
that I'm whistling hymns

Carla Sari

before leaving
my lips linger
on her forehead
'We'll meet again,'
I lie . . . to my sister

Carlos Colón

in the hospital
on the day I could have died
I catch up
on my unread books
and magazines

Carmel Summers

in the space
between your waking
and your leaving
those four quiet words
I wish I'd never said

Carmella Braniger

leaf-cutter ants
in my storybook
i pull out
the magnifying glass
for a closer look

Carol Pearce-Worthington

with the wonder
of a child and
now barely able to see
he remembers me
as beautiful

Carol Purington

this elegant gift
from a woman who told her son
not to marry me—
in so many ways
her taste impeccable

Carol Raisfeld

at papa's funeral
not an empty seat
except for one . . .
his worn prayer book
in my son's hands

Carole MacRury

yes, this too
could be my life
a few stones
mixed with bright bits of glass
left scattered on a grave

Carolyn Eldridge-Alfonzetti

above the chaff
old scarecrow with a hessian shirt
and painted smile
after all these years
your quirks still prickle

Catherine Mair

at the rest home she wakes
reaches out to touch my hair—
on the way home
we watch little diving ducks
ruffle the river

Catherine Smith

back page
of grandma's recipe book
how to
preserve a husband . . .
must have got the mix wrong

Cathy Drinkwater Better

nearly four decades
and you're still dead—
how silly of me
to think time
could undo mistakes

Chad Lee Robinson

if my brother had dreams
beyond his youth
he never spoke of them—
the river
still cold in June

Chen-ou Liu

long, narrow
aisle to the altar
the guests
stand on both sides thinking
they married the wrong people

mid-autumn night . . .
the wind whispers to me
Chinese words
that offer me a home
in the shape of a moon

walking out
in the middle of the lecture
on astrology
we saw summer stars
in each other's eyes

Cherie Hunter Day

a brown moth
folded on the windowsill
an expiration date
on my cereal box—
as if I needed reminders

a young man
contemplating freedom
no match
for the calla lily
with its continuous curve

Christina Nguyen

lady's slipper
one rare pink blossom
in June
my pregnant belly
finally shows

a stranger asks
have you decided
on baby's name?
screen door
banging in the wind

Claire Everett

the unquiet light
and silent song of snow
yet not awake—
even before they told me
I knew you were gone

stick thin and disjointed
colours barely scribbled in
without you
I am a child's drawing
of me

lobster pots
stacked at the quayside
nothing to catch
but a young girl's dreams
and the whispers of the tide

son of mine
what's done is done . . .
seed by seed, I'd breathe
back the dandelion clock,
place its stem in your hand

twisting and turning
a dragonfly splits
a ray of light . . .
he says he loves me
in his own way

Claudia Coutu Radmore

just as i begin
to find peace
in the center
of a tulip
he turns up again

a slice of tomato
warm from the garden
how dad loved it on toast
with only salt and pepper
and a daughter at his table

Colin Stewart Jones

winter light
licks the ebbing tide
beyond knowing
the sea answers back
in her own tongue

Collin Barber

while we talk
about God and the universe
another rock
from my slingshot
misses the moon

Curtis Dunlap

bread, wind, cheese,
the gentle patter of rain
on a new tin roof . . .
    come, read love sonnets to me
    and I'll read you Neruda

Cynthia Rowe

global warming—
the ship's prow fractures
ancient icebergs
while you fret about cubes
melting in your whisky

David Caruso

immortal
the moment
we caught each other's eyes
still teenagers
the homeless girl and i

David Platt

silence after storm
the standing stones sing
catching the song
but not an echo
of the understanding

David Rice

more lilacs
in the wine bottle
you've perfumed
each rainy day
of our vacation

David Steele

when she was sixteen
I showed her a kissing gate
and how it worked—
over sixty now I like
to check that she remembers

David Terelinck

autumn sunlight
strikes the stained glass
during prayer
you whisper
'malignant'

annual check up:
the doctor announces
perfect health,
the ache of your leaving
invisible in every test

Dawn Bruce

arms linked
in every travel photo . . .
the strangler vine twists
to the topmost reaches
of a dying tree

an owl flies
almost soundlessly
through the twilight . . .
my love's final journey
a long sigh, then silence

Dawn Colsey

caught by the camera
and garlanded with willow twigs
a piano floats on its back
the tsunami
playing its tune

Deborah P. Kolodji

thirty years
after your death
a quilt stitched
with fabrics
of my childhood

Dee Evetts

on the bus
putting up her hair
someone's hand
catches up the loose
strands on her neck

Diane Mayr

manual in hand
she watches the faucet leak . . .
dripdripdripdripdrip
no longer happy
to be single again

Dimitar Anakiev

a red sun rises
over the earthquake
tsunami & radiation
making the Emperor
speak to the homeless

Doreen King

as evening shadows
spread across the fields
I walk on slowly
spooked by the shape
of my life

Dorothy McLaughlin

family stories
photo albums, a name
on a gravestone
this is how my child
will know his father

Dorothy Walker

the warm breath
of moor ponies
sweet
as they share my apple
on a crisp Yorkshire morning

Dru Philippou

awakened
by crackles from a radio
a camper
discovers a night
of falling stars

Dy Andreasen

car wash—
young men from far away
polish . . . polish
their spent bodies
driven by the dream

Edith Bartholomeusz

first hint
of morning light
an owl
more shadow than bird
returns to the desert

clouds cast
shadows on the lake
and pass—
his coffin was white
and three feet long

Elaine Riddell

you look alarmed
when I mention my birthday—
I remind you
of the gift I helped you buy
and where you have it hidden

Elehna de Sousa

I wonder how
I never saw this stone before
in my backyard
a perfect
broken heart

Elizabeth Bodien

at my window
diminishing light
as on any day
I fend off the thought
of my own fading

Elizabeth Howard

dawn mountains
the colour of overripe plums
of old bruises
all that behind me now
I drive toward the light

Eve Luckring

Darfur:
even at this distance
I hear
the baby
crying at her breast

Fonda Bell Miller

family rings
adorn my fingers
the trees
near the sunlit river
ruby topaz gold

Francis Masat

cleaning his pool
our neighbor quietly curses
his key-limes
the neighbor's sea-grapes
but not our mangoes

Gary LeBel

along the way
they flare up behind my shoulder
all the little fires I started
and left behind
to smolder . . .

Gavin Austin

my mother sings
as she brushes her hair
of fine silver . . .
lament for the girl
missing from the mirror

Gennady Nov

they speak
to each other
the owl
in the cottonwood
and the far away train

Geoffrey Winch

on the horizon
yesterday the island
today only mist—
difficult at times
to remember an old friend's face

George Swede

difficult to
know others by
what they say—
smoke from chimneys
graying the sky

Gerry Jacobson

scribbly gum
growing out of solid granite
for two hundred years
pushing our roots down
into a hard land

sweeping
charcoal across the page
drawing
the swirling curves
of inner darkness

Giselle Maya

no one to hear
cherry petals scatter
seven times
the metal clang
of the morning bell

Grant D. Savage

those girls on the bus
their lively conversation
spilled peaches
rolling forward . . . and back
to me at each stop

Guy Simser

on his bedroom rug
counting seventy sit-ups
silently
from his dresser top looms
his credit card pre-paid urn

high school reunion
yes, after fifty years
each of us
has become
what we were

H. Gene Murtha

an iris
trapped in a vase
like love
there are things
we never wanted

Heather Feaga

starfish curve
texture of time
the sea
created me
to give you wishes

Hannah Mahoney

from a dusty box
his journal describes a day
I'd forgotten—
in the deep Arctic night
icebergs calve and drift

the nurse says
you'd better come now—
in the winter dawn
a wisp of cloud
floats across the moon

just this morning
the first magnolia buds
opening—
my mother's unwed initials
on the suitcase she brought east

Helen Buckingham

Mum calls
just to tell me
the sky is pink . . .
I peel back the curtains
with gratitude

Helen Yong

a gap between
frequent aftershocks
waxeyes feast
on pink camellias—
my heartbeat slows

Hortensia Anderson

roses cover
the tiny casket—
I touch my belly
how the emptiness
continues to grow

winter chill—
leaning over the infant
in her casket
i leave a dried rosebud
it too, will never bloom

Huguette Ducharme

along the thawing river
the slow movements
of the ice breaker
be patient, be patient
I tell myself

Ignatius Fay

popping corn
on the big wood stove
dad's stories
of growing up
in a tarpaper shack

Ikuko Melze

leaves of sumac
against late evening sun
shining deep red
the last glorious moment
trembling before the fall

Ikuyo Okamoto

Ikuyo Okamoto, Japanese-English translator

星空に
今宵は一つ
星増えて
我を見つむる
嗚呼、それは君

    hoshizora ni
    koyoi wa hitotsu
    hoshi fuete
    ware wo mitsumuru
    aa, sore wa kimi

        tonight
        the starry sky
        had a new star
        and it watched me
        ah, it was you

J. Andrew Lockhart

her beauty
leaves me as if
I'd steal it—
last gasp of winter
felt in the breeze

J. M. Rowland

the pine trees
on my neighbor's hill
are telling me
about the wind
that will be here soon

J. Zimmerman

thirty years later
holding hands at breakfast
coffee weaker
pancakes smaller
but the grasp still strong

James Tipton

I wave wildly
to the honking geese—
a neighbor
I never met
waves wildly back

Jan Dean

porridge on the wall
mashed veggies on the floor
ice-cream on the chair
sweet memories . . . how did they
grow so big on so little?

Jane Reichhold

grief
the tunnel of love
lengthened
by our moments together
swift passing days

Jan Foster

since the funeral
your old rocking chair
on the veranda
still creaks in the wind
 . . . unable to let you go

slow march
to a muffled drum
not the way
our warrior son
wanted to come home

my daughter has
a star named after her
enough light
for a mother's journey
through grief

Janet Lynn Davis

on bare ground
I sprinkle small seeds
with abandon
as if growing wildflowers
requires a lack of care

Jeanne Emrich

how he fussed
when I made him stand
for the silhouette
just so I could have
a shadow to love

Janick Belleau

Janick Belleau, French-English translator

À Kyōto
rendant visite
aux poétesses de waka—
se souviendra-t-on de moi
dans mille printemps?

> *in Kyoto*
> *paying a visit to*
> *waka poetesses—*
> *will I be remembered*
> *in one thousand springs*

Effluves de lilas
dans les ruelles vertes
plus de neige sale
je me lave le cerveau
de toutes idées noires

> *fragrance of lilac*
> *in green alleys*
> *no more dirty snow*
> *I wash my brain*
> *of all black thoughts*

Jeanne Lupton

her hair grows back
fine and soft
after chemo
cancer grows back too
so much to do, and nothing

between worlds
Mother hunches her shoulders
lifts her arms
sits up again and again
preparing to fly

in this old photo
see me standing in the shadow
of my father
ash, he casts no shadow now
and I struggle for light

Jeff Hoagland

on his belly
in our spring garden
my son teaches me
to see eye to eye
with the slugs

Jeffrey Woodward

I did not flinch but
closely weighed her every word
and only then walked out
as I'd walked in, alone
through a withered garden

Jim Schneider

gathered
we say the twenty-third psalm
but lose our way
in the valley
of the shadow of death

Jo McInerney

my daughter
almost a woman
in her voice
a child's inflection
when she calls my name

my dreams
always show you smiling
in a sunlit yard
glimpsed through the end door
of a dim passage way

Joanna Ashwell

one breath of wind
rattles the door
then a slow sigh
fills the house
gathering in the vacuum of you

Johannes S. H. Bjerg

looking
at a photograph
myself as a younger man
I can see
he had a future

my daughter's womb
round as the globe
she is walking on—
a little boy waiting
to come out and play

the room
where we said those words
caved in on itself—
I still crawl
through rubble

John Parsons

from house to house
our box of keys
old fuses   used plugs
I often wonder
what made you stay

old sanatorium
converted to flats
face at a window
in a far off wing
turns inwards

John Quinnett

sweeping away leaves
that keep on falling
the old woman
and her straw broom
slow-dance down the walk

John Samuel Tieman

I trust the autumn
the clarity of dying
oddly comforts me
a red leaf lands on my sleeve
it rests before moving on

John Soules

with you gone
I sleep in the spare room
with the dog
both needing the sound
of another's breath

Venus
rides shotgun above me
tonight
the ghosts of old lovers
lurk around the next curve

John Stevenson

both families
have their pariahs
the visible
and invisible
sides of the aisle

her note mentions
the blueberries blossoming
and the lettuce coming up
also, in passing,
chemotherapy

however young I was
when I stopped wanting
to stay up all night,
I knew it as a step toward death,
and felt it as a relief

Johnny Baranski

if only
I had kept it
the lottery ticket
on which you jotted
I love you

Joyce S. Greene

a silver ring
around the autumn moon
it may storm
but in our bed
he reads me love poems

one brown leaf
clings to a slender branch
not giving up
I leave a new message
on his voice mail tonight

Joyce Wong

like that Japanese
poetess of old, I know
what it's like
to dream behind closed doors,
to bloom in solitude

Judith Ahmed

no christmas tree
excitement gift-wrapped
or divine child
I wear my scarf
between two cultures

Jules Cohn Botea

Jules Cohn Botea, Romanian-English translator

Lan galben de grâu—
cu flori de mac în braţe
şi-n părul fluturând.
Cum eu nu am curajul
te mângâie doar vântul.

Golden field of wheat—
you have poppies in your arms
and in your fluttering hair.
As I don't have the courage
just the wind is hugging you.

Julie Thorndyke

bleached and dry
like the broken coral
on your desk
am I a mere keepsake
holding down our past?

Kala Ramesh

loneliness
isn't as bad
as having to face
fearful eyes staring back
at me in the mirror

dreams
fold into a bird
taking flight
the eyes of children
in the origami class

Karen Audioun Klingman

between
warmth of lit candles
an uninvited guest
whispers to the host
is no one else coming

Karen Peterson Butterworth

if these are
my autumn years
what will be my winter?
sudden blizzard or a
slow drawing in of days?

Kate King

hessian waterbag
hanging on the ute
far from home
your letters
slake my loneliness

Kath Abela Wilson

do siblings grow
like fragile leaves
on thin branches
over a shallow stream
so delicate some break

Kathe L. Palka

hunting wildflowers
I find indian pipes
doll's eyes and bee balm—
recalling all the names
my father taught me

my library filled
with books I hope to read
again
I fear I've planned
too far ahead

Katherine Samuelowicz

how is she
i wonder
this other me
living with my ex-husband
in this house we never bought

Kathy Lippard Cobb

on oxygen
mother lights
a cigarette—
part of me wants her
to explode

I wake to find myself
having a conversation
with you—
but there is only the moonlight
and four white walls

my baby photos
ruined in the flood—
pieces of me
lost somewhere inside
mother's failing mind

Keitha Keyes

wild violets
on my doorstep
uninvited
put down their roots
and welcome me home

I see one
and wait for the other
to land . . .
lorikeets mate for life
your intention was different

Kirsten Cliff

planning our wedding
in the hospital chapel
while I have chemo
I am not dying
but a part of me is

browsing
the second-hand books
from my wheelchair
today I decide
not to feel ashamed

re-negotiating
my drug regime
with the doctors
I tell them that today
they may see me cry

Kirsty Karkow

walking slowly
on autumn's oak leaves
I select one
brittle and brown
as the hand that lets it go

high on a hill
we fumble with buttons . . .
the earthy scent
as veils of a rare rain
sweep over arid land

I've been shown
many ways to love
over time
the next lesson
may be patience

Kozue Uzawa

kaleidoscope
I hold it against light
magically
they came into my sight
dark eyes of my dead lover

languidly
peony petals fall
into my heart's
empty space
after making love

Kozue Uzawa

Magdalena Dale, Romanian-English translator

Quietly
with a Chinese brush
I keep on writing
no one can go back
to the starting point

În liniște
cu o pensulă chinezească
continui să scriu
nimeni nu se poate întoarce
la punctul de la început

Larry Neily

reading on a tombstone
about an ancestor
crossing with the pilgrims—
at my feet among olive-tinted leaves
scented mayflowers

Laurence Stacey

another day
in the rat race
I grind
my last mandarin
into juice

explaining tanka
to my 5th grade class
a pivot
of laughter
from the hallway

LeRoy Gorman

health-conscious
she picks & orders
what's good for me
in the parking lot two gulls
fight over fries

Leslie Giddens

ancient wood
wraps its stillness
round my ageing body
in the clearing you wait
to hear me read your silence

Leslie Ihde

the day's
conversation revolves
on the potter's wheel
a vase the shape of anger
rises in my hands

Liam Wilkinson

reciting our lies . . .
I'll tell you I haven't
been waiting long
and you'll tell me
the traffic was murder

an evening stroll
at the edge of the sea
I toss the stones
I never knew
I'd been carrying

peering blankly
through the gates
of the old schoolyard
every child
I was

Linda Galloway

a skipping stone
begins its descent
to the bottom . . .
am I still a mother
now that my child is dead

rain drops break
a hydrangea into pieces—
my Tokyo friend
and I talk of our fathers
trying to kill each other

Linda Jeannette Ward

an old hag
bent over a shoulder bag
in the shop's window
I straighten my spine before
they can see it was me

bookshelf photographs—
an aunt I never see
a son seldom seen
the man I live with
who never sees me

no space provided
on her Bible's family tree
she writes in "divorce"
presses a primrose in
the Book of Revelation

Linda Papanicolaou

drawing our veils
against the sting of dust
and mothers' tears—
she and I divided
by the grief we share

Lisa Alexander Baron

flightless beetles
with useless wings sealed
beneath wing covers—
my daughter tells me
I worry too much

Lisa M. Tesoriero

weekend ritual—
the devout pray
in silence
waxing their surfboards
for the perfect wave

Liz Rule

the touch
once again of dew
on fallen leaves
quilting the silence
of your ever-sleeping child

Lois Holland

rainbow
sprung across the sky
arched prism . . .
how to bridge
the chasm between us

Lucas Stensland

she asks
if I want children
a breeze through
the half-open window
flips the calendar

the first time I saw
the Sistine Chapel
I was overcome
and briefly forgot
I was a virgin

Luminita Suse

rain sifted
through gossamer leaves
drop by drop
a thousand storms ago
I was dying to grow up

the dried leaf
in his poetry book
broken into pieces
his feelings for me
always a puzzle

mother's voice
on the telephone
an ocean away
seven hours older
her heart unchanged

Lynn D. Bueling

at sunrise
a bird sings outside
the hospital—
I look beneath the sheet
to where my leg used to be

Lynette Arden

a single brush stroke
on rice paper conjures
a songbird
now handled only with gloves
in the museum vault

M. Kei

all these socks
without mates,
yet not one
of them is willing
to pair up with another

she talks as she sails
the old wooden boat
of oyster days
and summer bays
and watermen grown old

Japanese quilting:
my mother and I
side by side
learning to stitch
deepest indigo

things that come
with the fog:
horseshoe crabs,
tall ships,
and wandering hearts

seven-eights
of a winter moon
perhaps it knows
how I feel
without a partner

Magdalena Dale

Mount Fuji
is cold and distant . . .
in vain
the cherries are in bloom
when you are not with me

Makoto Nakanishi

my students
graduated from University—
a block of sugar
in my tea slowly gets out of
shape in spring sunlight

Margaret Chula

the black negligee
that I bought for your return
hangs in my closet
    day by day plums ripen
    and are picked clean by birds

Kyoto nursing home
my last visit with you
uneventful
the sansanqua's
first white blossom

Margaret Conley

together
beaming for the camera
child and dog
knee-deep in floodwater
saving each other

Margaret Fensom

sea thunders
against the cliff
rain falls
on pine trees planted
for the fallen

Margaret Dornaus

searching
for meaningful work
between jobs
the chef spends his time
hand-feeding the birds

he says I speak
differently to strangers—
perhaps he can hear
the stilled whisper of love
in a mockingbird's song

Margaret Grace

in the market-place
a pile of red chillies
catches the light—
the blush on my cheeks
when your eyes meet mine

in a room
in my mind, a table seats
lost loved ones
sometimes I call the roll
and mother raises her hand

just once
would you come in daylight
and use the bell . . .
even the black bamboo's
shadow creeps through the door

Margaret Owen Ruckert

her biscuit of choice
and her mother's favourite,
'melting moments' . . .
the times the two disagree
on everything but taste

Margaret Van Every

cardboard boxes
containing all we were
in that prior life—
we ask ourselves
why open them

Margaret Van Every, Spanish-English translator

Raúl the gardener,
who speaks the language of flowers,
kneels among the callas
and asks why gringos
expect him to speak only English.

Raúl, el jardinero,
que habla la lengua de las flores,
se arrodilla entre los alcatraces
y pregunta por qué los gringos
lo esperan que hable sólo inglés.

Margarita Engle

country road
honey and mangoes
at a fruit stand
so many ways to taste
sunlight

after news
of the tsunami
wisteria
cascades
from every fence

Maria Steyn

the lightness
of daisies dipping
in the breeze . . .
today I will not think about
the weighing of the heart

a new friend
hesitates to share
her poetry
brings deep claret roses
and homemade jam instead

Marian Morgan

in the shell
of excess aging flesh
lives a young girl
still sun-baking on a beach,
still playing in the surf

Marian Olson

the grieving heart
is the loneliest lover;
tonight her poems
under a pool of lamp light
flow like her tears

Mariko Kitakubo

no one can tell me
at what moment it began
this sad story . . .
the endless winter
of my motherland

it'll be
my last love,
I'm telling
my late mother—
foot of a pale rainbow

assisted by Amelia Fielden

Marilyn Hazelton

family photo:
my father's father
before the booze
before the house was lost
before we inherited fear

my grandmother
steps away from sadness
to read tea leaves
a skill she learned
when everything changed

gold deepens
beneath the maple
more and more
I read obituaries
to start my day

how pitiful
old snow in sunlight
waiting
to return
to the sky

Marilyn Humbert

tomato vines
withered around their stake
at summer's end
clasping my stick tight
I shuffle down the hill

my son
waves goodbye . . .
in this moment
the last oak leaf
falls to earth

Marjorie Buettner

this strange absence
of all touch makes me feel
invisible
there are so many ways
a heart can break

Mark Holloway

telling me
her aches & pains
my elderly neighbour
stops, points
to the moon

Martin Lucas

summer
on the cusp of autumn
the man
who always walks alone
walking a dog

Mary Franklin

a mirror falls
and down its oval face
a crack appears—
in this fragile relationship
more bad times than good

Mary Kipps

a fairy princess
holds hands with a werewolf
their differences
forgotten on this night
of goblins and ghouls

Mary Lou Bittle-DeLapa

naked tree trunk
the shadowed curves looking
oddly erotic
another month
of living alone

Mary Mageau

he reads to me
'your presence is required
at the front line'
the sun disappears
behind grey clouds

beneath
the soldiers' honour roll
a scattered line
of poppies . . . like
a jagged red wound

Matt Quinn

I smiled at her
in the supermarket.
She smiled back
until the frozen turkey
fell from under her coat.

Matthew Caretti

from the bank
of the murky pond,
a flat rock
destined to become
just a single step

Max Ryan

woken on the eve
of my sixtieth birthday
by the sound of the sea . . .
the darkness out there
and the tug of an unseen tide

Maxianne Berger

heavy rain
turns the chrysanthemums
inside-out
for supper this evening
my ex and his husband

Mel Goldberg

please look again
where we stored our early days
among books and records
the happiness
must still be there

Melissa Allen

I lick a stamp,
pretending it's your cheek—
you taste like
every other boy I've ever
sent love letters to

branches scraping
on the bedroom window
you take pains
to mention your wife's name
from time to time

Merle Connolly

country town . . .
sheep and cattle
roam the hills
I wind back
my father's watch

Michael Ketchek

not everything
has to be explained—
sometimes at night
in your sleep you reach out
and touch my chest

Michael McClintock

what was beautiful
about the waterfall
was the fern
small and quiet
beside the torrent

like a bee I need
the scent of honey—
you've been gone
and I've been crawling
into your bed for naps

this spring
another man is tilling
my father's field—
I leave him alone
to his work

before discarding
the obsolete cell-phone
I looked inside
and poked with my finger
its dead electric heart

Michael Thorley

hardly used now
this little bush church
on a dusty road—
a sheep or two grazing
all that's left of the flock

he called it
going round the traps
for both
gathering the rabbits
and visiting family

she isn't there—
friends say to me
why then do I go
again and again
to her grave ?

Michele L. Harvey

the decision
about perpetual care . . .
a sparrow clings
to a laden seed head
of last year's grass

a whaleship
described as "world-wandering" . . .
where is the map
to chart the longing
of any man's heart?

Micheline Beaudry

Micheline Beaudry, French-English translator

December night
the words have frozen
the silence too—
in vain the lighted fire
in vain the poured red wine

nuit de décembre
les mots ont figé
le silence aussi—
en vain le feu allumé
en vain le vin versé

Mike Montreuil

my mind takes me
everywhere—
your skimpy dress
makes the voyage
so much easier

Mira N. Mataric

20 years later
alone
in our king size bed
I am your widow
still

Miriam Sagan

even she
couldn't quite explain
why she'd forgotten
the cello in the taxi—
autumn rain

Naomi Beth Wakan

bikini top
pinned to the notice board
all that is left
of long summer days
in Drumbeg Park

Paginini Jones

bare branches
only last year's pine
waiting for winter
echoing footsteps
and a creaking swing

Naoko Kishigami Selland

so proud
a girl on the front page—
the camera watching her
a radiation detector
sweeping over her tiny body

Noele Norris

the protective dragon
hugs her mountainous country
curls to hold it tight
and solidifies
into a great wall

Owen Bullock

spring is early
after an early winter
it's inevitable
that I should discover
an irregular heartbeat

she speaks highly
of the power of books
their place in her life
in all our lives
& throws them on the back seat

at the end
of the monk's chant
bells ring
a little boy says
well it's *definitely* tea time

Pamela A. Babusci

hair falling out
in clumps in my brush
on the floor
like petals
of a dying lotus

this morning dance
of who's right
who's wrong
i remember mother always
letting my father lead

Patricia Prime

I have worn out my grief
renewing it year after year
as loved ones pass
into memories and dreams
and silence that never ends

mother's grey skin
has become a long journey,
the ink of her veins
faintest white
a map of where she came from

a wall
full of photographs
these days I dust
the frames, wipe the glass,
scarcely see the faces

I dreamt you
came back last night
you were as young
and sure as you were then
but I was still my tired self

the girl presents
in three more or less equal parts——
dyed hair, tattoos, bare legs,
each one cross-referenced
with the other two

Paul Smith

it's my own name
I see
among the blossoms
scattered
on my father's grave

the corridor
was long and dark . . .
news of your death
closer
with each step

my son asks
what my father was like . . .
the weight
of telling him
I never really knew

avoiding the cracks
like I did back then
a little boy
willing his mum
to get well

trailing my hand
through the water
for a moment
more river
than man

Peggy Heinrich

strange, this life
no parents no mate no boss
to struggle against,
at night I fall asleep
to a chorus of frogs

this former lover
has slipped back into the cracks
in my life
what happens next,
mid-winter sun?

too young
my parents said
and when
the marriage fell apart
I never told them why

ten years later
her grave still lacks a stone
even when she was alive
no one in the family
could make her happy

Polona Oblak

so many places
I could have called home
yet I keep returning
to this shabby old flat
too small for two

although you
did not break my heart
departing swallows
each fall you take away
some of its shards

Quendryth Young

astride behind
my son on his Harley
wind on my smile
recalling him newborn
between my legs

Raffael de Gruttola

the cellist tunes
then re-tunes
for a slow adagio
on the evening news
another act of violence

Randy Brooks

so late for
headlights in the driveway
I decide to
hold on to the words
piling up inside

Renee Gregorio

winter, solitude
this scratch of pen on paper
much like the robin
her feet planted on snow
beak poking the frozen ground

Richard von Sturmer

dark blue sea
and underneath
sea cucumbers
the same blue, each
in its own universe

Roary Williams

no phone call
from the kids
he spends all day
fixing things
that aren't broken

Rie Ezaki

Enta Kusakabe & Tim Geaghan, Japanese-English translators

春の夜空に
星は増えたか
さらわれた幾万の命は
未だ波間に
漂っているか

Are there more stars
in the spring night sky?
Or are those swept lives
still drifting
between waves?

Robert McNeill

unaccustomed
to sounds of high-heels
on city streets
I spend the day
looking for horses

Robert Smith

sometimes
you have to just toss the words
into the stream
let the water decide
what the message is

Robert West

The real poetry
at the reading was nothing
the poet wrote, but
the long, slow dance of your hands,
the grace of their impatience.

Rodney Williams

young carver
of tribal totems
pressing his cheek
against the grain
of his forefathers

Ron C. Moss

in summer heat
a currawong settles uneasy
in the jacaranda tree,
falling embers from the fire front
glow and twist in the twilight

Ron Woollard

a distant star
coming and going
through the leaves—
all these promises
made to be broken

Rosemerry Wahtola Trommer

perhaps the moon
all along
has sung to me
in some crescent tongue
it thought I knew

Ruby Spriggs

a sudden loud noise
all the pigeons of Venice
at once fill the sky
that is how it felt when your hand
accidentally touched mine

Ruth Holzer

is it still
their anniversary
if one
has gone and the other
doesn't remember?

someone
has written my name
in this book
several times, as though
they secretly loved me

Saeko Ogi

Amelia Fielden, Japanese-English translator

繰り返し「悲愴」弾きゐしあの頃に曲り目に立
ち曲らむとせり

playing the Pathetique
over and over again—
that was the time
I was at a bend in the road
and about to turn

Sakurako

Enta Kusakabe & Tim Geaghan, Japanese-English translators

振り向けば
崩れた玄関に
仕舞い忘れた
雛人形
小さな金屏風が幸福の見納め

Looking back
at my tumbled entrance hall
dolls displayed for the Girls' Festival day—
A small gilded folding screen
was the last happiness I saw

Sanford Goldstein

my soul, I think,
can be sewn into a sail
and flung away,
yes flung into the ocean's deep
or under a patch of green

down
on my knees to clean
the kitchen floor,
that's the only relief
I have for this lonely week

she sat,
that sixty-three-year-old woman,
sat down uninvited,
all the words in her frail voice
somehow connected to my past

Sanjukta Asopa

sea-bound
this nameless river
carrying
a few broken twigs
and the ashes of Dad

Sarah Wika

cherry tobacco
drifts in through the window
my mother smiles
at things
I can't remember

Seren Fargo

forgetting the name
of the woman
who greets me—
a Viola glabella
nods in the wind

Sheila Sondik

first love
it took me years
to discover
what you said was true—
you were nothing special

Shernaz Wadia

the answer
is not in the "yes"
but in the way
your eyes move away
when you say it

Shona Bridge

his breath
through the didgeridoo
travels my spine—
there's nothing but pulse
and homecoming

bellbirds
like trinket drops
on ivory keys—
my mother nodfalling
in her favourite chair

Sonam Chhoki

in his drawer
old unused envelopes
addressed to me
what didn't father say then
that can never be said now

you put away the book
smooth out our yak-wool quilt
and close your eyes—
when it is for the last time
will I even be by your side

driving away
from the ancestral home
this thought . . .
tomorrow the early sun
will slant into my empty room

stillness of dew
on a nasturtium whorl
a breeze stirs . . .
if I could reach out and stop
my girl growing up so fast

Sonja Arntzen

that autumn
we slept under a sail
in a small dinghy,
woke to scatter a quilt
of yellow maple leaves

our desks share
the same study but we
are miles apart . . .
were it not for this solitude
I could not live with him

Spiros Zafiris

each cobblestone
of the old city stirs
ancient memories
add to this horse-drawn carriages
and we forget the year we're in

Stanford M. Forrester

while thinking
about the word
home . . .
i watch a hermit crab scuttle
over a crumbled sand castle

Stella Pierides

so here is the tree
of the liquid gold Homer spilt
so liberally—
between epic verses and
bare rocks it grows its olives

Steve Mangan

Saturday dad—
I wait outside the bookies
with a can of pop,
at church we light a candle
for his horse

Steve Wilkinson

born in poverty
struggling to survive
another day
he watches the setting sun
half hoping he'll see it rise

Sue Richards

a single strand of spider silk
flickers sunlight
up and down its length
my mind thinking
not thinking of you

Susan Constable

like question marks
bee stings cover my legs
each welt asking
what I did that summer
to make my father angry

the skin of a snake
shimmers with rainbows
even after death—
will the poems I leave behind
ever be as beautiful?

just a dot
standing on a glacier
or a speck
sailing across the ocean
yet this man can fill my world

Svetlana Marisova

downstream
drifting in my shadow
a single mayfly
and this moment marked
on the water with chalk

Sylvia Forges-Ryan

the professor drones
on and on about novels
of doomed love
I ask myself what
other kind is there

T. J. Edge

waiting room
how many more crayons
will turn to dust
before she completes
her father's portrait

Takako Nazuka

Enta Kusakabe & Tim Geaghan, Japanese-English translators

わずかばかりの
義援金
箱に投げ入れて
富豪でないことを
少し呪う

I throw a little donation
in the box
and a little curse
at myself
because I'm not a millionaire

Taro Aizu

picking ten pink roses
from our garden
I float them secretly
in the bathtub
for Mother's Day

I can neither see
nor hear it,
but time
flows through my body
like blood

after dark
magnolia blossoms
have appeared
in the twilight
like white lamps

Terra Martin

everything
in its proper place
but my heart
incompatible
with tidiness

Terry Ann Carter

nothing lives
in the wooden cage
only a memory
of a creature
who sang before dawn

Terry Ingram

the empty lot
where they held camp meetings
now a highrise
faint strains of songs
float in the rain

Tess Driver

she sells
her paintings for seed
to plant a crop—
after ten years of drought
the rain is falling

Tessa Wooldridge

at 92
and short of days
my neighbour
hands his garden's fruit
across our common fence

Tito

Night crossing—
Just beyond the armoured soldiers
Holding back the traffic
At the border gate,
Flower sellers.

Juarez, Mexico, 9.2.10

Tom Clausen

summer night
in a pile of rubble
the house's scent,
a hundred years
just like that . . .

even with new snow
we have an old talk,
the one where my part
is to answer correctly
what she wants to hear

Tomohime

Enta Kusakabe & Tim Geaghan, Japanese-English translators

まっ黒な汚泥を
さぐれば
腕時計、写真、イヤリング
潮干狩りのような
思い出探し

> *Digging into*
> *black dirty mud*
> *I found a watch, photos, earrings . . .*
> *seeking memories*
> *is like collecting clams*

Tracy Davidson

cut out of the will
all he ever left me
was a legacy
of broken bones
and unseen scars

Vasile Moldovan

Vasile Moldovan, Romanian-English
translator

În palma-ntinsă
a cerșetorului orb
în loc de bănuți
veniți pe neașteptate
cei dintâi fulgi de omăt

In the palm
of a blind beggar
instead of coins
the first snowflakes
arrived all of a sudden

Vasile Smărăndescu

Vasile Smărăndescu, Romanian-English translator

Ridic ciutura
să strâng cu mâna căuş
stele bob cu bob—
când vii la ceas de taină
le prefir în calea ta.

Water in the well
with my palm I skim the pail
to catch stars one by one—
when in the night you visit
I scatter them before you.

Veronica Shanks

from a roadside stall
fruit and spices
jam-packed in a jar
the lingering taste
of our last holiday

Victor P. Gendrano

Victor P. Gendrano, Tagalog-English
translator

the silent sound
of her absence
fills their room
only the echoes
of yesterday remain

napuno ang kanilang silid
ng tahimik na ugong
nang kanyang pagkawala
gunita ng kahapon
siya lang naiwan

Yūko Kawano

Amelia Fielden, Japanese-English translator

I want the body I had
before my illness,
the body of a woman
with the scent of earth
after the rain

I who laugh often
should be healthy,
but I am
a tumbled bucket
in the sunshine

lining up
all our household cleavers
I sharpen them
as I watch my daughter
silently sobbing

on a rainy night
it comes slithering
stealthily home—
oh dead child,
don't raise your head!

finally even I
have come to understand
that the smell
of family spirits
is the smell of burning earth

Tanka Prose

Florentine Studies

Charles Tarlton

morning in Florence
the shops still closed
before *Vespas* clog
the narrow streets
of the *Quattrocento*

When I visited Florence, Italy, in 1969, I stayed in a pension *altro Arno*, a huge house of red stone behind high walls. From the balcony of my room you could see into the garden of a neighboring convent and, then, up through the cypress trees, a section of the old city wall.

A very large green, blue, yellow, and red parrot lived along a rusted pipe that extended from the ground to the roof, running by all the rented balconies. He could hold on with both feet and scurry up and down the pipe to wherever there was food or interest. He talked incessantly.

from his perch
this old bird
an ancient bird
sings the same song again
always the same song

That year the Arno had overflowed. I was scheduled to view Machiavelli's letters and manuscripts in the *Biblioteca Nazionale Centrale*, but the library basement was still flooded and my visit cancelled. There I was in Florence for two weeks with no responsibilities at all. Sitting at a café in front of Michelangelo's David, I made plans.

In the *anfiteatro* at Fiesole a company from Rome was performing Machiavelli's play, *Mandragola*, a politically ironic and bitter sexual farce. Sitting next to me on the ancient stone slab seats was a professor of biology from the University of Florence. He spoke perfect English and, over a coffee during the break, he explained to me that the Italian (really Tuscan) of the play sounded old and distant to him, the way Shakespeare must have sounded to me. I told him that I really couldn't understand the Italian, anyway, but that I had studied the play so intensely in English that I always knew what was happening.

> Cesare Borgia
> once butchered enemies
> at a banquet—
> later at dinner
> I look for a corner table

> a child of *fortuna*
> Borgia tried to ride the wind
> over mountains
> not even Machiavelli's favorite
> was lighter than air

In the street where I was staying was a rosticceria where, for a couple of dollars, you could buy roast chicken, hearth baked green lasagna, and fried zucchini flowers. Around the corner you could buy a gallon or so of Chianti for another dollar. I thought about staying there forever.

Chianti is *vino dalle colline*
Arezzo, Pistoia, Siena, Pisa
Firenze-invented
in the hilly geography
of princely ambition

Up on the *Belvedere* I watched the fireworks on San Giovanni's feast day, as D. H. Lawrence had done, in dismay—flash boom, and confusion, ending in an orgasm of endless explosions. I looked around for Lawrence's frightened dog underneath the parked cars; he was not to be found.

~Florence, Italy

Unlocked

David Terelinck

The tumblers refuse to budge. I jiggle, withdraw and insert, and try again. Still nothing. I remove the old-fashioned key and feel the smoothness of it. Small, no longer than three inches. The head is a fine filigree pattern and resembles a four leaf clover. The metal, with brass coating almost completely worn away, is warm to touch. Despite the smallness, it sits heavy in my hand.

> thick dust
> on the glory box lid—
> I write her name
> foolishly thinking
> it will bring her back

I rummage through the laundry and find a can of degreaser. A short burst into the lock and I leave it long enough to boil the kettle. Once more I place metal to metal. The lock complains, but this time it does not refuse me entry. A creak of hinges and the stale rush of fifty years of her life envelop me.

> I make a pot
> too many
> memories
> to dilute
> in a single cup

Freeze-frames of her existence mothballed before me. Where does one begin? How do you catalogue a difficult and forgotten life? Delicately, like a surgeon harvesting for a skin graft, I remove the top layer. Slowly I peel my way back through her life. The years fall away, down into her youth, before she was my mother.

A bundle of letters, yellowed with the patina of her passing teens, finds its way into my hands. The once-pink ribbon is frayed. It slips easily off, slackened by the passage of time.

a voyeur
I peer into her past
shamelessly
searching for the proof
she never provided

Just words. No clues, no directions for where to turn next. Moving forward in her life, I search for the father I never knew. Like her, he remains a mystery. No name jumps out, no liaison slips into view. My knowledge of him remains inaccessible.

Another bundle of her past slips through my fingers. Twelve years of cards. All signed by me. Mother's Day, Christmas, birthdays. Handmade at school, and then store bought when I was old enough for a weekend job. She kept every one.

I wonder if she ever longed for a card from a lover. From the father of her son. Did he know about me? Did she know about him?

autograph book
filled with the names of people
I never knew—
when I sign my name
is this who I am?

Three hours later, I have trawled the length of her life. The catch is scant. I encoffin the remains of her and replace the lid. My tea has grown cold, along with the scent of my heritage. I am no closer to him, or to her.

I leave the chest
unlocked:
the treasures
I thought it contained
buried with her

Pursuit

Dawn Bruce

Ghosts and shadows intermingle through this love affair. At last we travel miles away. I change my name, he changes his occupation.

> before we met
> our life was lemon-ginger tea
> today
> the fragrance of jasmine
> drifts around us

The house we rent is in my new name, in a quiet, undistinguished neighbourhood. We don't need the entertainment of bars, theatres, dining out or even friends. Instead, he sketches while I write.

Some weekends we pack the car and set off for a bush holiday, camp under the stars and observe unspoilt nature going about her business in that keen yet quiet manner that is foreign to most humans.

I've begun to relax and shop at the weekend for exotic ingredients to follow recipes from his grandmother's old notes. He relaxes too, setting up a Japanese garden in the courtyard, water feature included. I'm delighted by his skill.

> in grey light
> of the coming dawn
> the phone shrills . . .
> we turn to each other
> and hold our breath

Art of Decay

Marie Lecrivain

To entertain ourselves, my best friend and I decide to attend an art exhibit at La Luz de Jesus Gallery. Tonight, there is a book signing and photographic exhibition of ossuaries and charnel houses. Having visited such places on trips to Europe, we're both curious to see what kind of art can be crafted from demise. As we drive through the worn out streets of East Hollywood, searching for a parking place, I look through the window for signs of the familiar places I used to know.

> the old neighborhood
> has been adorned
> in neon lace and jewels
> an artful illusion
> to hide decay

As we make our way to the gallery, we find ourselves surrounded by multi-generational goths. I glance at one woman, about my age. She has bright red hair, ghostly white makeup and dark-smudged eyes. Under the streetlights, I can see deep lines carved around her mouth and eyes, as well as the crepiness of her neck.

> a young girl's desire
> an old woman's reality
> are both welcome
> at the moment
> of Death's embrace

We make our way into the gallery. The photographer is in the corner, surrounded by admirers. The photos themselves are stunning: a Swiss saint's bones gilded with gold; a mummified infant swaddled in blankets forever sleeps inside an iron cradle. I find myself looking into the hollow eyes of a 19th century Bavarian skull, with the name of the deceased artfully written across its brow. This is my favorite. It speaks of veneration, of reverence. The photographer and the unknown artisan have transformed this icon of death into a symbol of hope.

as long as love
and skulls and bones
and names remain
no one will ever
be forgotten

Red Marble

Marilyn Hazelton

In rooms of El Escorial, the palace from which Felipe II directed the Counter Reformation throughout Europe, martyrs gaze toward heaven as blood streams from their wounds. Hand pressed hard to mouth, I pass the kind of depictions that sent me stumbling into the world decades ago, stripped of faith.

amid
art justifying
power
with little mercy
a cell phone rings

Somewhat later, I follow men and women in their Sunday best through the public entrance of Felipe's private cathedral. The guidebook in my hand tells me that my companions' stunted growth came from malnutrition during Spanish Civil War childhoods. At 5' 3", I am tallest, at 66, the youngest. Together we shuffle past a guard, his arms crossed, eyes half-closed. I am startled by the beauty of the ceilings and walls.

angels lift saints
toward heaven's blue
dazzle
so thinly painted
that good life

We wander down the main aisle to sit or kneel. A velvet rope divides sanctuary from pew. Steps of red marble veined with white, as if to remind the faithful of the body and blood of Christ, lead to the high altar. I remember that the basilica is modeled on descriptions of Solomon's Temple. Also, Felipe's Inquisition tortured or executed those accused of being "secret Jews".

in the Temple
remade as cathedral
belief
grips the hand
of doubt

A woman in a red and white dress, her hair tinted the color of sunset, pauses before the velvet rope. She reminds me of my mother years after giving birth to eight children. I watch, mouth open, as she slips beneath the flimsy barrier. Blending with the marble, flatfooted, she pulls herself up each of the seventeen steps. Finally, her back to the altar, she stands at Felipe's private entrance to the cathedral, the open door of his bedroom. From his bed, the dying king could see the host raised and chalice lifted.

each morning
bread and wine
transfigured
what did that ritual
have to do with living?

This intruder in a gaudy dress raises her arm and waves Hello!!! to a ruler described as keeping "his smile and his dagger" very close. What can I do but adopt her as *una madre?* She turns, renavigates steps of privilege and slips beneath the rope. As the guard walks rapidly down the aisle in panic, *mi madre española* pats her hair, smoothes her dress, and rejoins her friends.

> neither
> saint nor martyr
> I rise
> to light a candle
> for all spells broken

~El Escorial, San Lorenzo, Spain

Tanka Sequences

Lighted Mirrors

Elizabeth Howard

chiseled from granite
the elderly schoolteacher—
in icy dawn, she shuffles
up the garden path,
teeth gritted against pain

she clips the item
with precision
he places it in the laden box
nodding as if to say
it's a husband's duty

in the lighted mirrors
the starched white shirt
blinds her
to his ashen face
and palsied hands

hearing the old lady's words
it's easier being his widow
than it ever was
to be his wife
I fill in the details

in her feverish dream
he placed in her hands
a shattered redbird
when she came to herself
she knew the bird bore his name

Shawbridge Youth Centre formerly "The Boy's Farm and Training School" (est. 1901)

Angela Leuck

"angel" wall clock
with white wings
& halo
my son
in juvenile detention

leaving the city—
bright waving fields
of goldenrod
all the way
to the prison

walls, ceiling, floor
painted white
still the gloom
of my son's
prison cell

pacing behind
the barbed wire enclosure
teenage boys
instead of panthers
and tigers

in a locked unit
my son
talks of flying
to South America
when he gets out

his math exam
rescheduled
my son calculates
the height
of the prison fence

the young blonde
prison guard
in short shorts
says firearms
are her passion

behind barbed wire
my son tells me
he now has
his escape plan
all figured out

stepping into
this new role
of prison mom—
I wear sunglasses,
consider cutting my hair

my son
now a high school graduate
I ride
the big yellow school bus
home from the prison

What the City Whispered To My Grandmother

Kath Abela Wilson

in her small room
far from the river
I watch her
serenely she builds
her own pyramid

always on the watch
at the back window
she prays
for what
will happen next

she lets down her hair
in a net of hail marys
they climb back up
land on the roof
to keep her awake

her blue and pink
canvas of day
feeds the night
always about
to arrive

behind the sheer curtain
alligators
are always waiting
we catch the whispering city
in our mouths

Editor Biographies

M. Kei is a tall ship sailor and award-winning poet. He lives on the Eastern Shore of the Chesapeake Bay (USA) and apprenticed aboard a skipjack, a sail-powered oyster dredge. He now serves with a fully rigged ship. His publications include over 1400 tanka poems in six languages and ten countries. He is the editor-in-chief of the anthology series, *Take Five : Best Contemporary Tanka*, and the author of *Slow Motion : The Log of a Chesapeake Bay Skipjack*, Recommended Reading by the Chesapeake Bay Project. He edits *Atlas Poetica : A Journal of Poetry of Place in Contemporary Tanka*. He is the compiler of the *Bibliography of English-Language Tanka*, which documents over one thousand publications from 1899 to the present day. He is also the author of the award-winning gay Age of Sail adventure series, *Pirates of the Narrow Seas*.

Patricia Prime, a semi-retired early childhood teacher, lives in Auckland, New Zealand. She is co-editor of *Kokako*, reviews editor of *Takahe*, and reviews/interviews editor of *Haibun Today*. Patricia has been one of the editors of the *Take Five* anthologies since their inception. Her poems, reviews, literary essays and interviews have been published in the *World Poetry Almanac* (Mongolia) and in various journals. She is currently writing collaborative tanka sequences with an Australian poet and shisan renga with poets from Europe and also from New Zealand. Her work is scheduled for publication in *Haibun Today, Contemporary Haibun Online, Lynx, Atlas Poetica, Gusts, Eucalypt, multiverses* and *red lights*, among others.

Magdalena Dale was born in, and lives in, Bucharest, Romania. She is a member of the Romanian Society of Haiku and World Haiku Association. Her work has been published in several reviews and anthologies in her country and abroad. Her tanka and haiku have appeared in more literary sites online. She wrote a bilingual tanka book *Perle de roua/Dew pearls*, a bilingual renga book *Mireasma de tei/ Fragrance of* *lime* with Vasile Moldovan and a bilingual haiku book *Ecourile tăcerii/ The echoes of silence."* She received several awards for her work.

Amelia Fielden is an Australian professional translator and an internationally awarded and published tanka poet. Seventeen books of her translations of modern and contemporary Japanese tanka have appeared over the last 11 years, with a further two volumes forthcoming in 2012. Amelia has also published six collections of her own tanka, the most recent being *Light On Water* (2010). She has collaborated with other Australian poets to produce four books of responsive tanka,including *Yesterday, Today & Tomorrow* (2011) with Kathy Kituai, and the bilingual *Words   Flower* (2011) with Saeko Ogi. Amelia is happy to be contacted at anafielden@hotmail.com.

Claire Everett's haiku, tanka, and more recently, haibun and tanka prose, have appeared in many of the short-form poetry journals worldwide. She was a contributing poet for cycle 11 (spring/summer 2011) of the online journal *Daily Haiku*. Claire's interest in tanka prose increased when she was invited by M. Kei to conduct an in-depth interview with Jeffrey Woodward for *Atlas Poetica 9* (July, 2011) discussing the history and practice of tanka prose. She is now delighted to be the tanka prose editor for *Haibun Today*. Claire lives with her husband and five children in North Yorkshire, England, and draws most of her inspiration from walks on the Moors and Dales and in the Lake District.

Owen Bullock's first tanka appeared in *tangled hair* in 2000, and thereafter in *Eucalypt, Lynx, Magnapoets, Modern English Tanka, Moonset, paper wasp, Atlas Poetica, Presence,* etc. He has published a collection of haiku, *wild camomile* (Post Pressed, Australia, 2009); fiction, *A Cornish Story* (Palores, UK, 2010), and poetry, *sometimes the sky isn't big enough* (Steele Roberts, New Zealand, 2010). Owen has edited a number of journals, including *Kokako* and *Poetry NZ*. He is currently on the International Editorial Board for the online journal,

Axon: Creative Explorations (University of Canberra). He teaches creative writing online for the Waiariki Institute of Technology and the New Zealand Writers' College. <http://www.owenbullock.com/>

David Terelinck (Sydney, NSW, Australia) is a full-time employee and part-time writer who seriously wishes the balance were reversed. He has been involved in creative writing for more than twenty-five years with many awards for his short stories, articles and poetry. David has been writing tanka for the past five years and has been widely published in international tanka journals. David's first tanka collection, *Casting Shadows*, was published in late 2011. During the same year, David co-edited *Grevillea & Wonga Vine: Australian Tanka of Place*, with Beverley George. He enjoys giving tanka and other creative writing workshops, and lives by his motto *scribo ergo respiro*. In 2012 he is looking forward to joining the editorial panel of the Canadian journal, *Gusts: Contemporary Tanka*.

Janick Belleau's latest publication *D'âmes et d'ailes / of souls and wings* – a bilingual tanka collection won her the Canada-Japan Award in 2010. She edited the collective work *Regards de femmes – haïkus francophones* in 2008 and coedited *L'Érotique poème court / haïku* in 2006. Her feature articles and presentations in Canada, in France and in Japan deal with the contribution of women in the advancement of haiku and tanka. Her website is <http://www.janickbelleau.ca>.

David Rice lives in Berkeley, California, with his wife and aging dog. Three children and three grandchildren also live in the Bay Area. He has been reading and writing tanka for more than twenty years, and his poems have appeared in numerous anthologies. He has self-published two tanka chapbooks and, with Cherie Hunter Day, the collaborative tanka sequence *Kindle of Green* (2008). In 2012 he became the editor of *Ribbons*.

Venues Consulted, 2011

To be eligible for consideration, a work had to be finished, available to the general public, published during 2011, and verifiable. Abbreviations in credits are annotated here.

Print Periodicals

Albatros : The Journal of the Constanta Haiku Society. [ALBT] Constanta, Romania, 2011.

Atlas Poetica : A Journal of Poetry of Place in Contemporary Tanka. [ATPO] Perryville, MD: Keibooks, 2011.

Blithe Spirit Journal : Journal of the British Haiku Society. [BLTH] London, UK: British Haiku Society, 2011.

bottle rockets. [BTLR] Windsor, CT: bottle rockets press, 2011.

Caltech Poetry Club Journal. Pasadena, CA: Caltech, 2011.

Eucalypt : A Tanka Journal. [EUCL] Pearl Beach, AUS, 2011.

GUST : Contemporary Tanka. [GUST] Burnaby, BC: Tanka Canada, 2011.

Haiku Bindii. [HBIN] Adelaide, AUS: Bindii Japanese Genre Poetry Group, 2011.

*Haiku Canada Rev*iew. [HCRV] Napanee, ONT: Haiku Canada, 2011.

Haiku—Magazine of Romanian-Japanese relationships / Revista Haiku. [HKRO] Bucharest, RO: Romanian Haiku Society, 2011.

HPNC Newsletter. [HPNC] San Francisco, CA: Haiku Poets of Northern California, 2011.

Kokako. [KOKA] Te Atatu South, Auckland, NZ, 2011.

Lilliput Review. [LILR] Pittsburg, PA: Lilliput Review, 2011.

Magnapoets : taking over the world one poem at a time. [MAGP] Tecumseh, ONT, 2011.

Mariposa. [MARI] San Francisco, CA: Haiku Poets of Northern California, 2011.

Moonbathing—a journal of women's tanka poetry. [MONB] Eldersburg, MD: Black Cat Press, 2011.

Paper Wasp. [PAPW] Chapel Hill, Queensland, AUS, 2011.

Presence. [PRES] Preston, UK, 2011.

red lights : a tanka journal. [REDL] Allentown, PA, 2011.

Ribbons : Tanka Society of America Journal. [RIBN] Baltimore, MD: Tanka Society of America, 2011.

The Tanka Journal. [TTJ] Tokyo, JP: Nihon Kajin Club: The Japanese Tanka Poets' Society, 2011.

Time Haiku. [TMHK] London, UK: Time Haiku Group, 2011.

Valley Micropress. [VLMP] Whiteman's Valley, NZ: n. p. 2011.

Anthologies

Anemones. [ANEM] Giselle Maya, ed. Saint Martin de Castillon, France: Koyama Press, 2011.

Art and Alchemy. [ARTA] Kath Abela Wilson, ed. Pasadena, CA: Poets on Site, 2011.

Awakenings : The Art of Susan Dobay. [AWAK] Kath Abela Wilson, ed. Pasadena, CA: Poets on Site, 2011. [first edition]

Butterfly Away : Magnapoets Anthology Series 3. [BFAW] Antonovic, Aurora, ed. Tecumseh, CAN: Magnapoets, 2011.

Garden Mandela. [GDMD] Giselle Maya, ed. Saint Martin de Castillon, France: Koyama Press, 2011.

Dreams Wander On : Contemporary Poems of Death Awareness. [DRWO] Robert Epstein, ed. Baltimore, MD: MET Press, 2011.

Food for Thought. [FOOD] Amelia Fielden, ed. Port Adelaide, AUS: Ginninderra Press, 2011.

Grevillea & Wonga Vine : Australian Tanka Poetry of Place. [GAWV] Beverley George & David Terelinck, eds. Pearl Beach, AUS: Eucalypt, 2011.

Lighting the Global Lantern. [LTGL] Terry Ann Carter, ed. Maple Plain, MN: Wintergreen Press, 2011.

Many Windows : Magnapoets Anthology Series 4. [MYWD] Antonovic, Aurora, ed. Tecumseh, CAN: Magnapoets, 2011.

Montreal Zen Poetry Festival. [MZEN] Montreal, CAN: Mother Tongue Bookstore, 2011.

One World, Many Voices. 2011. [1WMV] Santa Cruz, CA, 2011. [concert] <http://www.youtube.com/watch?v=uNdC7xnkofo>

Pacific Asia Museum's 40th Anniversary Audio Tour. [PA40] Kath Abela Wilson, ed. Pasadena, CA: Pacific Asia Museum, 2011. <http://www.oldflutes.com/poetsonsite//pam-audio-tour-2011.htm>

Painted My Way : the Exhibition of the 14th Annual Henry Fukuhara Workshop APC Fine Arts and Graphics Gallery. [PTMW] Kath Abela Wilson, ed. Pasadena, CA: Poets on Site, 2011.

Mother Tongue Bookstore Reading, [MTBR] Ottawa, CAN, April 7, 2011.

Tanka Huddle. [THDL] Julie Thorndyke, ed. Sydney, AUS: Swan Bay Books, 2011.

Contests

Haiku Poets of Northern California. *San Francisco International Competition : Tanka Contest.* [SFIT] San Francisco, CA: HPNC, 2011.

3rd Kokako Tanka Competition. [KOKA-3] Te Atatu South, Auckland, NZ: Kokako, 2011.

Spirit of Japan Tanka Contest. [LPPT-2011] 2011. <http://lyricalpassionpoetry.yolasite.com/2009-world-tanka-contest.php>

Tanka Society of America. *International Tanka Contest 2011.* [TSAI-2011] Baltimore, MD: Tanka Society of America, 2011. (Published in RIBN)

Works by Individual Authors

Amelia Fielden & Saeko Ogi. *Words Flower from One to Another. Carindale, AUS: Interactive Publications Pty Ltd, 2011.*

Angela Leuck. *Suddenly a Desire : Rose Tanka.* Carleton Place, CAN: Bondi Studios, 2010.

Anna Martineau Merritt. *Life, In Other Words*. Morrisville, NC: Lulu Enterprises, 2011.

Beverley George & David Terelinck. *Tanka Calendar*. AUS: George & Terelinck, 2011.

David Terelinck. *casting shadows : collected tanka*. Alexandria, AUS: Cedar Press, 2011

Edith Bartholomeusz. *Aglow at Noon : Selected Haiku and Tanka*. Eldersburg, MD: Black Cat Press, 2011.

Eric Spangler, composer. *Five Levels of the Watershed*. Annapolis, MD: Chesapeake Bay Youth Orchestra, 2011. [music] <http://soundcloud.com/dubble8/five-levels-of-the-watershed-1>.

Gerry Jacobson. *Stillness Moves*. Braddon, AUS: New Territory Press, 2011.

Helen Buckingham and Angela Leuck. *Little Purple Universes : Tanka*. CAN: The Literary Factory, 2011.

Jane Kohut-Bartels. *White Cranes*. Morrisville, NC: Lulu Enterprises, 2011.

Julie Thorndyke. *Carving Granite*. Port Adelaide, AUS: Ginninderra Press, 2011.

Katherine Samuelowicz. *We Made Each Other Up : tanka, haibun, & haiku*. Mt. Gravatt Qld, Australia: Post Pressed, 2011.

Katie Batten MacDowell. *Into Quiet*. Morrisville, NC: Lulu Enterprises, 2011.

Kathy Kituai & Amelia Fielden. *Yesterday, Today & Tomorrow*. Queensland, AUS: Independent Picks, 2011.

Kozue Uzawa. *I'm a Traveler*. Baltimore, MD: MET Press, 2011.

Larry Kimmel. *Collected Poems 1968-2008*. Colrain, MA: Winfred Press, 2011.

Liliana Negoi. *Footsteps on Sand*. Morrisville, NC: Lulu Enterprises, 2011.

Margaret Van Every. *A Pillow Stuffed with Diamonds : Tanka on La Vida Mexicana*. (revised) Tallahasee, FL: Librophilia, 2011. [Spanish-English]

P. K. Pradhy. *The Tiny Pebbles*. Allahabad, India: Cyberwit.net, 2011.

Paul Smith. *Tanka Poems*. 2011. <http://www.youtube.com/watch?v=vORrulBJ43c&noredirect=1>

Pentti Olavi Syrjälä. *Silent Tanka. Some Examples from the book - Hiljaisuuden tankoja*. 2011. <http://www.youtube.com/watch?v=uh__lOhbgHA.> [Finnish-English]

Pentti Olavi Syrjälä. *Tanka on Sandskär Island part 1*. 2011. <http://www.youtube.com/watch?v=W0tbBOCWWt4> [Finnish-English]

Pentti Olavi Syrjälä. *Tanka on Sandskär Island part 2*. 2011. <http://www.youtube.com/watch?v=bFz1ZGgABYQ&feature=related> [Finnish-English]

Sálongo Lee. *Sálongo Lee*. 2011. <http://www.youtube.com/watch?v=xd6tWxtOwXl>

Sonja Arntzen & Naomi Beth Wakan. *Reflections: response tanka*. Carson City, NV: Pacific-Rim Publishers, 2011.

Taro Aizu. *The Lovely Earth*. Morrisville, NC: Lulu Enterprises, 2011.

Yūko Kawano. *The Maternal Line*. Amelia Fielden & Saeko Ogi, trans. Baltimore, MD: MET Press, 2011.

Websites and Online Journals

7x20 Journal of Micropoetry. [7x20] 2011. <https://twitter.com/7x20>

140 Max. [140M] 2011. <http://www.140maxmagazine.com>

25 Tanka for Children (and Educators). [25CH] M. Kei, ed. Perryville, MD: Keibooks, 2011. <http://AtlasPoetica.org>

25 Tanka Poets from Great Britain and Ireland. [25GB] Jon Baldwin, ed. Perryville, MD: Keibooks, 2011. <http://AtlasPoetica.org>

25 Tanka Prose. [25TP] Bob Lucky, ed. Perryville, MD: Keibooks, 2011. <http://AtlasPoetica.org>

Agonia—Ateliere Artistice. 2011. <http://english.agonia.net/index.php>

American Tanka. [AMTK] 2011. <http://www.americantanka.com>

Androxa. 2011. <http://androxa.wordpress.com/2011/08/07/romanian-tanka/>

Ardea. 2011. [ARDE] <http://www.ardea.org.uk>

Chrysanthemum. [CHRY] Austria, 2011. <http://members.aon.at/bregen>

Contemporary Haibun Online : A Quarterly Journal of Contemporary English Language Haibun. [CHO] 2011. <http://contemporaryhaibunonline.com>

Daily Haiga : An Edited Journal of Contemporary & Traditional Haiga. [DLHG] Spring Lake, AL: n. p., 2005-.1918-851X <http://dailyhaiga.org>

A Eucalypt Challenge : Coining a Word. [EUCL-COI] Beverley George, ed. Pearl Beach, AUS: Eucalypt, 2011. <beverleygeorge@idx.com.au>

A Eucalypt Challenge : Year of the Rabbit [EUCL-RAB] Beverley George, ed. Pearl Beach, AUS: Eucalypt, 2011. <beverleygeorge@idx.com.au>

Eye to the Telescope. 2011. [EYET] <http://eyetothetelescope.com/current.html>

Fall Romance : Romance under a Waning Moon. [FRUW] Ray Rasmussen, ed. 2011. <http://raysweb.net/fallromance/>

From Lime Trees to Eucalypts: A Botany of Tanka. [FLTE] Angela Leuck, ed. Perryville, MD: Keibooks, 2011. <http://AtlasPoetica.org>

Gogyohka on the Disaster in Japan. Kusakabe Enta & Tim Geaghan, eds. & trans. [GODJ] *Flashquake*, 2011. <http://issuu.com/cindybell/docs/flashquake_vol10_iss4/search?q=gogyohka>

Haibun Today : The State of the Art. [HBTY] 2011. <http://haibuntoday.com>

Haiga of the Month. [HGMN] 2011. <http://haiku-wortart-forum.de/Forum24-1.aspx>

HaigaOnline : A Journal of Poetry and Painting. [HGOL] 2011. <http://www.haigaonline.com>

Haiku News. [HKUN] Laurence Stacey & Dick Whyte, eds. 2011. <http://www.wayfarergallery.net/haikunews>

a handful of stones. 2011. [HFST] <http://www.ahandfulofstones.com/>

Ink Sweats and Tears : the poetry & prose webzine: Haibun, Haiku & Haiga. [INKS] 2011. <http://ink-sweat-and-tears.blogharbor.com/blog>

Introducing Tanka Poetry to the World. 2011. http://introducingtankapoetrytotheworld.blogspot.com/

Jars of Stars. [JARS] 2011. <http://jarsofstars.wordpress.com>

Lavender Review. 2011. <http://home.earthlink.net/~marymeriam/Lavender>

Lynx: a journal for linking poets. [LYNX] Gualala, CA: AHA Poetry. 2011. <http://AHAPoetry.com>

mango moons. [MNGM] India: Secunderabad, India: Muse India, 2011. <http://museindia.com/focuscontent.asp?issid=37&id=2671>

microcosms. [MCSM] 2011. <http://Twitter.com/microcosms>

The Minnow : Journal of Haiku & Other Short Form Literature. 2011. <http://theminnow.org/taika.php>

Muse India : a literary ejournal. [MSIN] Secunderabad, India, 2011. <http://www.museindia.com>

New Verse News. [NVNW] 2011. <http://www.newversenews.com>

Notes From the Gean : A Journal of Japanese Short Forms. [GEAN] 2011. <http://geantree.com/index.html>

One Hundred Gourds : A quarterly journal of haiku, haibun, haiga, & tanka poetry. [100G] 2011. <http://www.haikuhut.com/ahg/index11.html>

Prune Juice : A Journal of Senryu and Kyoka. [PRUJ] 2011. ISSN 1945-8886 <http://www.prunejuicejournal.com>

Scifaikuest. 2011. <http://www.samsdotpublishing.com/scifaikuest/contents.htm>

Simply Haiku : A Quarterly Journal of Japanese Short Form Poetry. [SH] 2011. <http://www.simplyhaiku.webs.com>

Sketchbook : A Journal for Eastern and Western Short Forms. [SKBK] 2011. <http://poetrywriting.org/Sketchbook0-0Home>

Tanka Corner. [TKCR] 2011. <http://lyricalpassionpoetry.yolasite.com/modern-tanka-corner.php>

TankaNetz. 2011. <TankaNetz.de>

Tanka Online. [TKOL] 2011. <http://tankaonline.com>

tinywords : haiku & other small poems. [TINY] 2011. <http://tinywords.com>

Tobacco Road. 2011. <http://tobaccoroadpoet.com>

Blogs, Personal Pages, Miscellaneous Online Works

Alan Segal. *Old Pajamas.* 2011. <http://oldpajamasfromthedirthut.blogspot.com>

Alex von Vaupel. *Alex von Vaupel dot com. 2011.* <http://alexvonvaupel.com>

Alexis Rotella. 2011. <http://alexisrotella.wordpress.com>

Alison Williams. *Miso Soup.* 2011. <http://haikusoup.blogspot.com>

Angela Leuck. *A Poet in the Garden*. 2011. <http://www. acleuck.blogspot.com>

Angie LaPaglia. *Earthgirl*. 2011. <http://myearthgirl. blogspot.com>

Annette Mineo. *Sea Stone Poetry*. 2011. <http://seastone poetry.blogspot.com>

Bonfire Field : Just another WordPress.com weblog. 2011. <http:// bonfirefield.wordpress.com>

Brian Zimmer. *Kirigirisu*. 2011. <http://myku-brian. blogspot.com>

Cady Ford. *An Exploration of Poetry*. 2011. <http:// poetexplore.blogspot.com>

Carol Johnston. *Dog and Pony Poetry*. 2011. <http:// morganabag.blogspot.com/>

Chen-ou Liu. *Poetry in the Moment*. 2011. <http://chenouliu. blogspot.com>

Chiyuki Yanase. 2011. <http://chicolateflavoredsong.blogspot.com>

Christina Nguyen. *A wish for the sky : Haiku, tanka, and other short form poetry*. 2011. <http://tina.mnnguyen.com>

Claire Everett. *At the Edge of Dreams*. 2011. <http:// thosethr3words.wordpress.com/>

Clive Martyn. *A writer's story*. 2011. <http://biddingfor business.blogspot.com/search/label/haiku>

Collin Barber. *Haiku, Tanka, Haiga & Haibun*. 2011. <http:// collinbarber.com/45.html>

Coyote Sings, aka Roary Williams. *My Dreams Move Slowly*. 2011. <*http*://mydreamsmoveslowly.tumblr.com>

Cross-Leaved Heather. 2011. <http://www. haikuheather.blogspot.com>

Curtis Dunlap. *Tobacco Road Blog*. 2011. <http://tobacco roadpoet.blogspot.com>

Deborah P. Kolodji. *Poetry Scrapbook and Random Musings*. 2011. <http://dkolodji.livejournal.com/241869.html>

Edjo Frank. *Edjo Frank's Blog*. 2011. <http:// edjofrank.wordpress.com/>

Eric Houck. *Haiku, Tanka, Senryu, Haiga*. 2011. <http:// www.ericshaiku.blogspot.com>

Fay Aoyagi. *Blue Willow World*. 2011. <http://fayaoyagi. wordpress.com/category/tanka>

H. Gene Murtha. *Miller's Pond : The Poetry of H. Gene Murtha*. 2011. <http://hgenemurtha.blogspot.com>

J. Andrew Lockhart. *Past Tense : A Collection of Haiku, Tanka, Haiga, and Other Forms of Poetry*. 2011. <http://james alockhart.blogspot.com>

J. S. H. Berg. *Scented Dust*. 2011. <http://scenteddust. blogspot.com>

J. S. H. Bjerg. 2011. *Lines5*. <http://lines5.wordpress.com/>

Jane Kohut-Bartels. *Lady Nyo's Blog*. 2011. <<http://ladynyo. wordpress.com/>

Jenny Ward Angyl. *The Grass Minstrel*. 2011. <<http://grassminstrel. blogspot.com/>

Joanne Morcom. 2011. <http://www.joannemorcom.com>

Kay Tracy. 2011. <http://immersedinword.blogspot.com/>
Kayo. *Haiku Poems of Kayo of Japan.* 2011. <http://kayo2011. blog100.fc2.com/>
Liam Wilkinson. *Liam Wilkinson dot com.* 2011. <http://www. liamwilkinson.com>
Lilliput Review Blog. 2011. <http://LilliputReview. blogspot.com>
Listening to the Wind. 2011. <http://thewindknows.blogspot.com>
M. Kei. *Kujaku Poetry & Ships.* 2011. <http://kujakupoet. blogspot.com>
Magdalena Dale. *Tanka Dream.* 2011. <http://tankadream. blogspot.com/>
Mariko Kitakubo. *Tanka Poet Mariko Kitakubo.* 2011. <http://tanka. kitakubo.com/english>
Mark Holloway. *Beachcombing for the Landlocked.* 2011. <http:// thefragmentworks.blogspot.com>
Matt Morden. *Morden Haiku.* 2011. <http://mordenhaiku poetry.blogspot.com>
Matt Quinn. *PoemBlaze Blog.* 2011. <http:// poemblaze.wordpress.com/>
Megan Arkenberg. *White Cherryblossoms.* 2011. <http:// whitecherryblossoms.blogspot.com>
Miriam Sagan. *Miriamswell.* 2011. <http://miriamswell. wordpress.com>
Owen Bullock. 2011. <http://www.owenbullock.com/tanka.html>
Paul Smith. *Paper Moon.* 2011. <http://tanka-papermoon. blogspot.com>
Peter. *expatinCAT's Blog.* 2011. <http://juca2.wordpress.com/>
Peter Wilkin. *Peter Wilkin's Blog.* 2011. <http:// peterwilkin1.blogspot.com/>
R. K. Singh. 2011. <http://rksingh.blogspot.com/>
Robert D. Wilson. *A Lousy Mirror.* 2011. <http://lousymirror. blogspot.com>
Roswila. *Dream and Poetry Realm.* 2011. <http://roswila-dreamspoetry.blogspot.com>
Svetlana Marisova. *t'heart of haiku.* 2011. <http:// theartofhaiku.com/svetlana/svetlanas-tanka.html>
Terry Ingram. *Signs of Life.* 2011. <http://tdi.posterous.com/>
Taro Aizu. 2011. *The Lovely Earth.* 2011. <http://blogs.yahoo.co.jp/ lovelyearth_mont> [Japanese-French-English]
T. J. Edge (ten ten ten). *Last Ammonite.* <http:// tententen.posterous.com/>
Vince L. Wilson. *What's In Vince L. Wilson.* 2011. <http:// vincewil.posterous.com/>

Credits

Credits abbreviated to save space. Complete citations may be found in the List of Venues Consulted (above).

Adelaide B. Shaw. if I could turn back, REDL 7:1.

Akiko Hasegawa. a bunch of daffodils, GUST 14.

Alan S. Bridges. halfway through spring, FLTE.

Alan Summers. sometimes, 7x20.

Alex von Vaupel. at night the hospice, ATPO 9.

Alexander Ask. white quartz stone, GUST 14.

Alexis Rotella. I left before I fell, PRUJ 5; Up before dawn, Alexis Rotella blog.

Alison Williams. how many things, Miso Soup.

Amelia Fielden. capricious spring, KOKA 14; from Europe, BFAW; she leaned there, Yesterday; the corsages, MAGN 8.

André Surridge. from a hilltop, VM 14:3.

Andrew Riutta. when I was eight, GEAN 3:3.

Angela Leuck. 'Shawbridge Youth Center.' ATPO 8; alone in the house, Little Purple; In an old picture, Ibid; he always knows, MONB 4; walking home, Suddenly.

Angie LaPaglia. crouching by the fire, Earthgirl; the weight, ATPO 10.

Anita Virgil. primordial soup, EUCL 11.

Anne Benjamin. a simple sack, THDL; this morning, GUST 13.

an'ya. an icy wind, SH 8:3; together we may, DLHG; cold cemetery, Tobacco Road Poet.

Antoinette Libro. overnight ferry, REDL 7:1.

Askold Skalsky. passes me in the hall, SKBK 6:4.

Aubrie Cox. the silence between us, 'Cicada Chorus,' ATPO 10; summer leaves, EUCL.

Audrey Olberg. arriving home each night, GUST 14; at last, REDL 7:1

Autumn Noelle Hall. Chinese characters, RIBN 7:3.

Aya Yuhki. the river in the shade, TTJ 39.

Barbara A. Taylor. a grateful mother, SH 8:3.

Barbara Robidoux. midnight drive home, MONB 3.

Barry Goodmann. low tide, MARI 23.

Beatrice van de Vis. opening a window, MONB 4.

Becky Alexander. sickle moon, MONB 3.

Belinda Broughton. generations, HBIN 1.

Bett Angel-Stawarz. crushed eucalypt, HBIN 1.

Bette Norcross Wappner. from the eaves, MONB 3.

Beverly Acuff Momoi. the cat retreats, SH 9:2; the magnolia's, EUCL 10.

Beverley George. it's not the new, THDL; passages you marked, RIBN 7:1; this blue balloon, MAGN 7.

Bob Lucky. a beggar, PRUJ 5; prayer flags, CHRY 9.

Brendan Slater. a mattress, RIBN 7:1; in this foreign land, PRES 43.

Luminita Suse. rain sifted, MYWD; the dried leaf, Agonia; mother's voice, ATPO 10.

Lynn D. Bueling. at sunrise, RIBN 7:1.

Lynette Arden. a single brush stroke, HBIN 1.

M. Kei. all these socks, TKCR; she talks as she sails, Five Levels of the Watershed; Japanese quilting, Kujaku Poetry; things that come, Ibid; seven-eights, FRUW.

Magdalena Dale. Mount Fuji, BFAW.

Makoto Nakanishi. my students, GUST 13.

Margaret Chula. the black negligee, LTGL; Kyoto nursing home, MONB 3.

Margaret Conley. together, GAWV.

Margaret Dornaus. searching, SH 9:1; he says I speak, RIBN 7:3.

Margaret Fensom. sea thunders, HBIN 1.

Margaret Grace. in the market-place, SH 9:2; in a room, RIBN 7:3; just once, Third Place, KOKA Tanka Contest.

Margaret Owen Ruckert. her biscuit of choice, FOOD.

Margaret Van Every. cardboard boxes, ATPO 8; Raúl the gardener / *Raúl, el jardinero*, A Pillow Stuffed with Diamonds.

Margarita Engle. country road, GUST 14; after news, RIBN 7:2.

Maria Steyn. the lightness, GUST 14; a new friend, EUCL 11.

Marian Morgan. in the shell, GAWV.

Marian Olson. the grieving heart, MONB 4.

Marie Lecrivain. 'Art of Decay.' HT 5:4.

Mariko Kitakubo. no one can tell me, EUCL 10; it'll be, TTJ 39.

Marilyn Hazelton. 'Red Marble.' 25TP; family photo, SH 9:2; my grandmother, SH 9:2; gold deepens, MAGN 7; how pitiful, SH 8:3.

Marilyn Humbert. tomato vines, FOOD; my son, KOKA 14.

Marjorie Buettner. this strange absence, 'Losing the Way,' 25TP.

Mark Holloway. telling me, Beachcombing for the Landlocked.

Martin Lucas. summer, GEAN 2:4.

Mary Franklin. a mirror falls, SH 9:2.

Mary Kipps. a fairy princess, REDL 7:1.

Mary Lou Bittle-DeLapa. naked tree trunk, MONB 4.

Mary Mageau. he reads to me, 'Anzac Day,' ATPO 8; beneath, GUST 13.

Matt Quinn. I smiled at her, PoemBlaze.

Matthew Caretti. from the bank, 'Thus Spoke,' SKBK 6:6.

Max Ryan. woken on the eve, EUCL 10.

Maxianne Berger. heavy rain, GUST 13.

Mel Goldberg. please look again, PAPW 17:3.

Melissa Allen. I lick a stamp, PRUJ 6; branches scraping, EUCL 10.

Merle Connolly. country town, GAWV.

Michael Ketchek. not everything, REDL 7:2.

Michael McClintock. what was beautiful, GUST 14; like a bee I need, FRUW; this

Index

Educational Use Notice

Keibooks of Perryville, Maryland, USA, publisher of the anthology, *Take Five : Best Contemporary Tanka, Volume 4,* is dedicated to tanka education in schools and colleges, at every level. It is our intention and our policy to facilitate the use of *Take Five* and related materials to the maximum extent feasible by educators at every level of school and university studies.

Educators, without individually seeking permission from the publisher, may use *Take Five : Best Contemporary Tanka* as a primary or ancillary teaching resource. Copyright law "Fair Use" guidelines and doctrine should be interpreted very liberally with respect to *Take Five* precisely on the basis of our explicitly stated intention herein. This statement may be cited as an effective permission to use *Take Five* as a text or resource for studies. Proper attribution of any excerpt to *Take Five* is required. This statement applies equally to digital resources and print copies of the journal.

Individual copyrights of poets, authors, artists, etc, published in *Take Five* are their own property and are not meant to be compromised in any way by the anthology's liberal policy on "Fair Use." Any educator seeking clarification of our policy for a particular use may email the Editor-in-chief at Keibooks@gmail.com. We welcome innovative uses of our resources for tanka education.

Keibooks
P O Box 516
Perryville, MD 21903
<http://AtlasPoetica.org>

12529363R00138

Made in the USA
Charleston, SC
11 May 2012